HOW TO SURVIVE AS A WORKING MOTHER

A Practical Guide

Judith M. Steiner

KOGAN
PAGE

First published in Great Britain in 1989 by Kogan Page Limited, 120
Pentonville Road, London N1 9JN.

British Library Cataloguing in Publication Data

Steiner, Judith M.
    How to survive as a working mother.
    1. Great Britain. Working mothers
    I. Title
    305.4'3'0941

    ISBN 0-7494-0083-8
    ISBN 1-85091-928-3 Pbk

Typeset by The Castlefield Press, Wellingborough, Northants.
Printed and bound in Great Britain by
Richard Clay, The Chaucer Press, Bungay

Contents

fair *110*; Food – hers, yours, and the children's *114*;
Family life and the au pair *115*; Friends, neighbours and
the au pair *118*; Leaving and remembering *119*

Author's note

In this book I refer to the child very often as 'he'. Feminists, don't be offended. I have done this for three reasons. First, continuously writing he/she is silly; second, I want to distinguish the mother 'she' from the child; and third, I am the mother of two sons so I am afraid I naturally found myself writing 'he'.

Where I have written about mothers and new babies, I include adopted babies and children.

My thanks are due to all the kind people and organisations who provided information, answered my questions, and permitted the reproduction of copyright material.

Would the reader please note that the London telephone area code changes on 6 May 1990, and 01 will become either 071 (central area) or 081.

Chapter 1

Preparing for the Baby

Man works from sun to sun,
Women's work is never done.

Some years ago, an American scientist published an article in *Scientific American* showing that, on average, American women spend 59 hours a week on 'housework'. American women, by and large, possess every labour-saving device known to man from the trash compactor to the indispensable electric pencil sharpener. It must be assumed that British women spend at least an equal amount of time slaving away over the home and family.

The study was possibly embarked on to find out why working women seem so permanently exhausted. Let us assume a full-time working woman spends 40 hours a week at her place of work. By doing a swift calculation, you can see that this leaves her absolutely no time whatsoever for anything else.

	Hours per week
Working	40.0
Travelling	10.0
Toilette	6.5
Housework	59.0
Sleep – 7½ hrs per night	52.5
Hours used	168.0
7 × 24 =	− 168.0
Time remaining	0 hours per week

How does she do it? When does she do it? What does she do with the children?

Women go out to work because they want to go out to work, despite the fact that they already have a job at home. For most women, the job at home, despite its demands in time and labour, doesn't count. It doesn't count because society says it doesn't count.

Women with jobs are identified by their jobs alone. Only paid labour, it would appear, is valued. Unpaid labour is not only not valued, it is invisible. Young mothers, exhausted by the daily grind, are utterly demoralised.

Carole, a single mother, tells us why. 'It's degrading, isn't it, if you're doing something and it's a bloody hard job and it's difficult and it's classed as nothing because you're a scrounger because you're doing it. What does that do to your morale?'[1]

The term 'working mother' has come to mean only a mother with a job. This infers that taking care of the family, running a house, managing the domestic chores and responsibilities, organising and running the children's day, cooking, shopping, and running the household accounts is not work. A woman today would have to be wholly impervious to society's pressures on her not to seek a separate identity outside the home.

Women's jobs

Women tend to take jobs that fit in with their family obligations in terms of convenience and flexibility, and not jobs that match their own particular training or talents. Until a few years ago, working mothers were expected to fit in with the timetables of industry and productivity, employers having little knowledge or concern about the family responsibilities of their female employees. However, this situation is gradually improving as women achieve a higher profile in the workplace and employers are desperate to retain their skills and loyalty.

Women in fast-lane careers tend to work right through their pregnancies up to the expected week of confinement, and then return to work fairly quickly thereafter. They fear that they will fall behind their peers in their chosen profession if they indulge themselves in a career break for the child-bearing years.

Exhaustion

These women also reported feeling absolutely exhausted, particularly in the year after the birth of the first child. They also said they resented feeling so tired, but would not have considered giving up their jobs. The stress of being constantly tired and harassed leads to irritability and all the women said that the most important health factor in their lives was the value of a good night's sleep. Certain

1. *Double Identity: Lives of Working Mothers*, Sue Sharpe, page 42, Penguin, 1984.

adjustments have to be made in order to have the energy to bear the extra load of baby and home. Social life suffers but should be more than compensated for by the new baby.

The need to prioritise, say 'no' to unnecessary demands on their time and energy, eat well, sleep well, not drink very much and keep fit was paramount in their minds.

When a mother finds herself giving in to irritability and tension, she tends to blame herself, despite her resourcefulness and invention in sorting out the demands on her, instead of recognising that she doesn't have a proper framework of support to fall back on. All the mothers interviewed stressed the importance of a strong back-up in the form of help: a carer, a cleaner and a husband or partner.

Dressed for success and shrouded in guilt

Women are hounded through the pages of the popular press to 'have it all', as though it were not only possible but easy to set and fulfil personal goals of a blissfully happy marriage, a life-long close relationship with wonderfully gifted and loving children, and an extremely satisfying, highly paid, exciting job. Perfect woman, the fantasy of the mother you wanted yourself, *circa* 1950, has been supplanted by 'Superwoman', the wonder creature who can have and do everything.

The resulting emotional dilemma of never being able to be everything you want to be to everyone is called 'guilt'. Every woman I spoke to who had actively chosen to pursue a career experienced some feelings of self-doubt and guilt. It is a guilt that acts as a two-edged sword: the mother is damned if she gives up her career and damned if she doesn't. If she gives up her career she will have let herself down. If she doesn't stay at home with the children, she will have let them down.

Mothers looking for a childcarer should not consider that they are looking for a substitute mother, secretly worrying that they are abandoning their responsibilities. Instead, they should be seeing their career as additional to themselves. If you feel yourself a better person for working, once back at the office with the stimulus of work, the feelings of guilt will start to dissipate, if only to some extent. It is essential to develop a positive attitude and come to terms with feelings of guilt, counterbalancing the sense of loss with a sense of gain. Everyone experiences ambivalent feelings and doubts about doing the right thing.

For men, marriage, family and a career are complementary activities, without conflict. For women, they represent a terrific dilemma wherein compromises have to be constantly made. Many men feel resentful because their wives are too exhausted to cosset them and pander to their needs – some men need 'mothering' as well. This adds to the burden of guilt.

Children believe, because the mother is the initial care-giver and their first bond is with her, that mothers have the option of going out to work or not. They don't question the father's absence during the day. If all the other mothers they see in their lives have jobs, they are unlikely to question your job. However, if they find mothers waiting at the school gate for all their friends, while the au pair or the nanny waits for them, they will both question your being away from them and use it as a weapon.

Your child has every right to have feelings about your working, contrived or not, depending on the age of the child, which you neither can nor should ignore. Acknowledging the feelings and recognising that they are there doesn't make the feelings go away. But then, why should they go away? There is no way of getting round the fact that daily maternal departures are sometimes going to distress your child. Understand and respect the child's feelings. He has a perfectly legitimate right to object to your leaving. However, you have a perfectly legitimate right to go.

Feelings of guilt can take many different forms.

The superwomen complex

Not measuring up to a self-imposed standard of super efficiency is a common complaint. A few years ago a culinary reactionary to labour-saving devices in the kitchen wrote a book promoting the idea that food tastes better if it is made from scratch. 'Throw out your magimix, cut those carrots by hand, don't be caught in the supermarket with a cake mix', was the message. At about the same time the Princess of Wales gave birth to Prince William and, fully equipped with a staff of 300, dressed him entirely in hand wash, hand iron, Edwardian baby gear. A thousand crazy Sloane Rangers rushed out and bought pure cotton smocked baby dresses and dry clean-only nappy covers. Pay no attention to this nonsense. Wash-and-wear baby-grows are what babies are really comfortable in.

If your four-year-old wants to bake a cake with you, use a mix. Throw an egg in. All he wants to do is watch the beaters go round, stir the mix a little bit and eat it. When things are complicated, always think there must be an easier way. It isn't possible to have your house always ready for the photographer from *Homes and Gardens*. Suit your real self and family, not the superwoman image or anyone else's expectations.

Omnipresent mum

Your child knows very clearly and has known since he was very small, at a maximum of six or seven months, who his mother is and who the carer is. No mother is physically with her child all the time unless he is strapped to her back and she is out toiling in a field. You hired the carer because you have confidence in her. It's very important that you listen to her recounting the child's day at the end of it, but the first steps your child takes are the ones *you* see. Your child is a separate person and in the same way that you would not expect to know everything about another person, you will never know everything about him. Your carer will know more about your child than you do. Allow the carer to get on with it and by all means acknowledge that it is a hard job and that you respect it. You are not missing your child's childhood. You are giving him a different sort of childhood experience.

My wonderful child

If you are not at home to harass your children with a daily round of lessons, the sounds of the 2½-year-old next door practising the Suzuki method on his miniature violin will strike a blow at the very heart of your feelings of inadequacy. Children develop at different rates and speeds and in different directions. It is so easy to alienate your own child badly by trying to keep up, lesson-wise, with the Joneses. Find out what your child is interested in. It is easy to think your own child is lazy because he doesn't want to do what you want him to do. Or to decide he is without talent because he isn't interested in following the pursuits you followed as a child. Find out what he is interested in and let him follow those interests, and then you will have a wonderful, and happy, child. Also, how many great Japanese violinists can you name?

Eat together as a family

Be grateful if you are greeted with 'Hi Mum, when's dinner?', or its variation, 'Hi Mum, what's for dinner?' Sitting down together as a family for the evening meal is one of the most important parts of family life. With busy working parents and children who are studying, it is sometimes hard work to actively be a family. Dinner time is a good time to practise. As soon as the children are old enough, get them used to the ritual of setting and clearing the table, even if the table you use is only an arm's length away from the cutlery drawer. It's less work for you and creates a routine. Meal-times are the best opportunity for communication a family has.

Sadly, so many families have given up the family dinner altogether. The children are losing out on essential social training and everyone is losing out on simply getting to know each other. It is even worse to sit together eating with a television carefully positioned and turned on so that no one has to pay any attention to anyone else. From this children learn that they shouldn't share their feelings, that no one is interested in them, and that the passive stimulus of the television is much more important than the family in the room. Some lesson!

Try not to turn dinner-time into a nagging session. It is very easy to concentrate on what is wrong rather than what is right. Try to put aside the direness of the table manners or the disastrous school report. Listen to the children. Children, particularly teenagers, often complain that adults aren't remotely interested in their views on anything and only ask them what they think so they can interrupt and deliver a lecture on the subject. Have dinner together as often as possible, don't nag and listen.

The Lego trap

Do board games bore you to tears? Does building with Lego drive you round the bend? Can you not wait to get back to the office on Monday morning? Every mother has to work within the context of her own personality. You have to make some concessions to small children and play with them in ways they enjoy and understand, but it should not become a punishment and torment for you. On the other hand, it isn't reasonable never to get down on your hands and knees and make no concessions. Compromise.

Lots of extras that I never had

The mother who gets home in the evening at 10 pm and compen-sates for her feelings of guilt by providing her child with endless expensive toys, stays in summer camps and wonderful holidays isn't really compensating the child at all. The largesse is a way of allaying her own guilty feelings for not being there.

Hallmark Cards in America is cashing in on the guilt feelings of absentee parents with a series of saccharin cards to leave around the house for their children to find. If you have had to leave the house for a 7 am breakfast meeting, you can leave a card under your child's cereal bowl that reads, 'Have a super day at school'. If you know the late meeting followed by dinner is not going to get you home before midnight, 'I wish I were there to tuck you in' left on your child's pillow is supposed to comfort him and assuage your guilt at the same time. I doubt it. Go down this road and you will find it filled with land-mines by the time your child is a teenager.

It will get easier as they get older

The process of bringing up children is filled with wonderful breakthroughs. Just when you thought she would never be able to dress herself, there she is, one brown sock, one blue sock and overall back to front, but she did it all by herself. Suddenly bed-time, while losing some of its charm, speeds up immeasurably. Little Johnny presents himself bathed and in his pyjamas ready for his bed-time cuddle. No sooner is she brushing her own teeth and tying her own shoelaces than she is walking to school on her own. Blink once and he is carrying his own house-keys.

Don't delude yourself into thinking that's it. The less demanding children are physically, the more demanding they become emotionally. This is when you find out the real meaning of being a parent. Children, from birth until long after they leave home, need attention and counselling. Growing up is hard to do and through each and every milestone in a child's life, parental guidance is essential. You have got to take the time to listen, remember what it was like being 12 or 15 or 18, and help. When children become teenagers, they have to make choices in every area of their lives from academic work to their social lives that will affect the rest of their lives. Abandon them at this stage, assuming that all the raising is finished, and you, and they, will pay a heavy price.

The myth of 'quality time'

A few years ago the concept of quality time appeared, promoting the idea that you could gear the smaller amounts of time you spend with your children to such a high level that the quality made up for the time limitations. It is an attractive idea that only takes your needs into account and totally ignores your child's.

So-called quality time imposes a pace on the child that has nothing to do with his needs. Because you are away from your child more than you are with him, you will not respond as easily or naturally to his moods. A highly pressurised two hours removes all spontaneity, produces tension and is doomed to failure. Imagine that you come bursting in the door, ready for your magical two hours and your child ignores you entirely. 'Oh, my God', you think, 'I forgot to kiss him good-bye this morning and he's punishing me.' In truth, only you noticed or remembered that you forgot to kiss him good-bye this morning, and at the moment he is wholly concentrating on a puzzle he is doing, or he is on his stomach watching a spider make its way along the skirting board. He is not going to be pleased at being interrupted. The overstimulation of quality time can lead a child to withdraw into himself. What children thrive on is the pressureless hours of just being. If he doesn't acknowledge you, sit down, open a newspaper, wait for him to finish what he is doing, and be the warm and loving body waiting for a cuddle. He won't let you down.

Leaving a sick child
This is the worst problem for a working mother. Little children become ill suddenly and not infrequently. You have to make arrangements that are practical and make sure your child knows that you really care and are doing the best you can. Dealing with an ill child is covered thoroughly in Chapter 11.

The best time to have a baby

Look at the women pushing the push-chairs. Never risk making an embarrassing *faux pas* and compliment someone on her lovely grandchild or her smashing baby sister. Regardless of whether she looks as if she should be receiving Child Benefit or Retirement Benefit, ten to one, she is the baby's mother.

The best time to have a baby is when you are expecting one and want it. The professional mothers I interviewed had all had their children in their late 20s or early 30s. One mother, a psychiatrist, had had her first baby at 43. The non-professional mothers had had their families younger, thereby fulfilling the stereotype of the mother getting her child-rearing years behind her at an early age, leaving her with almost 30 years, unfettered by the responsibilities of young children, in the world of work. The older mothers had established their careers in their 20s, but then found they had to step out of the fast lane for a while until their children became a little more independent.

None of the mothers said they had planned their lives that way. I don't believe it is possible to plan a career in terms of when you are going to marry and have children. Emotions cannot be brought out and put away to order.

Once the baby is on the way, as well as considerations about your job, there are certain things you have to consider regarding how, post baby, you are going to manage your life.

One major factor you must obviously take into careful consideration is what you actually have the room for. Where are you going to put the maternity nurse, the nanny or the au pair whom you have your heart set on? Is she going to sleep on the pull-out sofa in the living room? Are you all going to share the same bathroom?

Unfortunately, no one offers employer training on how to organise someone in the home. The chapters on nannies and au pairs will fill you in on what you should expect and how to relate to live-in help. Whether you have a personality that is adaptable to living with a stranger in the house and, equally important, how disruptive the presence of live-in childcare is going to be to your husband or partner, is very important.

If you are an experienced employer, you will not be likely to find it stressful to have to organise the carer's day, give instructions, praise work well done and criticise tactfully work inadequately done, generally making your needs and wishes known. If, on the other hand, you have no previous experience of management, life with live-in help can be hell if not handled properly.

Examine yourself very carefully and discuss the matter of what kind of help you are going to employ thoroughly with your partner. If you know you and your husband to be private people who would be distressed or unnerved by having someone else in the house, consider a daily nanny, a minder or a day nursery.

Once you become a parent, you are a parent for life, and your life will never, I repeat, never be the same again.

Do not take approaching parenthood lightly. Organise yourself accordingly. Make arrangements for childcare as far in advance as possible. Social Services Departments often frustrate long-term planning by refusing to give you the names of minders more than a few months before you need one, because they don't want minders to be tied down by a baby who might be late in arriving or a mother who changes her mind. Most agencies take the same attitude, based on experience that babies seldom make their first appearance when originally expected and mothers often change their minds. Nurseries tend to start telephoning from the top of a waiting list when they have a vacancy and fill it with the first positive commitment. Be sure to put yourself on that waiting list.

Think through the options, do your own research and feel

confident and prepared. Don't allow a situation to develop where you are expected back at work within the week, and you are still dithering about the childcare arrangement.

Childcare options and what you should expect to pay

Childcare is not tax deductible so anything you pay is out of taxed income. A company subsidy for a workplace nursery is taxed out of income like any other perk. If your company operates a voucher scheme for childcare, vouchers that are not exchangeable for cash are free from National Insurance contributions (NICs), although taxed like other vouchers as part of your income.

So you have to think in terms of an outlay in post-taxed income. If you are paying £60 per week for out of the home childcare, you must think in terms of the £3120 (52 weeks × £60) plus the tax you pay on that. If you are considering live-in help in the form of a nanny or mother's help you have to add on employer's NICs. A fully qualified NNEB (National Nursery Examination Board) nanny being paid a gross salary of £6893 per annum will cost you £7,513 once you have paid the NICs. An au pair doesn't pay tax or NICs but at £25 per week will cost you £1,300 post-tax income. You must also consider not only the obvious expense of food but all the hidden expenses in your electricity and gas bills for heating, laundry, hot water for endless baths, and the telephone. If you run a car to enable her to ferry the children about, you will spend over £1000 per annum on insurance, maintenance, road tax and petrol.

Also, think in terms of time, energy and space. If you have a bedroom to spare, you can accommodate live-in help. Only a maternity nurse would accept sharing the bedroom with the baby. Stepping over the nanny camped on the pull-out sofa bed in the living room is not a reasonable proposition. Consider carefully how much help you need in running the house besides childcare. If you have a nanny, you must also be able to afford a cleaning woman, or do it yourself. A nanny is not available in the evening to help you peel the potatoes and clear away the dinner dishes. An au pair or mother's help is, but you are trading in your privacy for an extra pair of hands at the end of a working day. Think in terms of combining costs, particularly if you have more than one child. For example, if you have a mother's help at home and an older child in a nursery, you may find your outlay is greater than if you had a full-time nanny.

On the other hand, you may feel the stimulation of the nursery is worth the extra expense, and the mother's help does the work a separate cleaner would cost. If you are working part time, the hours and contribution of an au pair might be enough. What you decide is the most convenient, economical and workable for you depends on your financial and physical resources.

In addition to the costs of an extra person in the household, expect to pay the following:

Maternity nurse

A maternity nurse is almost always an NNEB and sometimes a fully qualified infant nurse. She will stay for up to six weeks, but no longer than three months.

Cost: £180–£240 gross per week.

Nanny

A nanny should be over 18 and preferably have an NNEB training from a college of further education or a diploma from a bona fide nanny college such as Norlands. She works all day but does no housework. Her role is to take care of the children only and manage things in the house that pertain exclusively to the children's well-being.

Cost: £110–£140 gross per week.

Mother's help

This is the general term for an untrained English-speaking girl, usually British or Commonwealth, who may either aspire to becoming a nanny when she has more experience or simply may find being a mother's help a secure and convenient job to do in foreign parts.

Cost: £65–£100 gross per week.

Au pair

Au pairs are girls from 17 to 27 without dependants, usually from Europe, who want to stay in Britain for a year to learn English. They are expected to work five hours a day or 30 hours a week doing light housework including care of the children. An au pair is not suitable for a family where both parents go out to work.

Cost: £25–£30 per week.

Baby-sitter
Cost: Totally dependent on your area and age of sitter. £3.50 per hour is the top rate in London SW1.

Childminder
Women, usually between 18 and 55, who must be registered with their local Social Services Department to care for no more than three under-fives, including children of their own. Do not leave your child with an unregistered minder. The charges are set by the minder herself and relate to the going rate in the area. The hours of care provided are arranged between parent and minder.

Cost: Varies from £40–£65 per week, depending on the part of the country, London not necessarily being the most expensive.

Local authority nursery schools and classes
These are often attached to the primary school provided by the local education authority. Children from three years of age (rising four to five) usually start part time and graduate to full time as they get older.

Cost: Provided by the education authority and there is no charge to the parent.

Local authority day nurseries
These are provided for children from nine months to five years. Because of the cuts in spending by local authorities in recent years, these are, by and large, restricted to children of families with a special need for this care and children who are considered to be at risk. They provide full-time care from 8 am to 6 pm.

Cost: Varies and heavily subsidised. Can be as low as £8–£10 per week.

Workplace nurseries
Very rare and very expensive. An employer subsidises places in the nursery taken up by members of its staff, and the nursery might even be in the same building or close by. Children are usually

accepted from 0 to 5, with the correct staff ratio, 1 to 3 for babies, 1 to 5 for toddlers. If the nursery is run by a local authority for its staff or is in a hospital for its staff, it is usually not too expensive. They provide year-round care, usually from 8 am to 6 pm.

Cost: Depends entirely on the subsidy of the employer. Anything from £35 to over £100 per week.

Privately owned day nurseries

The new ones, set up as commercial enterprises, are more expensive than those that have been around for a long time, often second generation family businesses. Open 50 if not 52 weeks a year, for children from 0 to 5. They have qualified staff in the statutory ratios.

Cost: £60 to over £100 per week.

Community nurseries

These are run like the local authority day nurseries from 8 am to 6 pm, the difference being in the manner of funding, which is by a grant, usually from the local authority.

Cost: Depends on area but usually between £8 and £10 per week.

Playgroups

These can be either privately run or voluntary non-profit making organisations of parents who can choose to join the Pre-School Playgroups Association by payment of membership and the adoption of a constitution recognised by the Charities Commission. There is always a play leader and each parent pays anything from 25p to £1 for a session. Sessions last for approximately 2½ hours and children can join in for anything up to five sessions a week.

Cost: Depends on whether it is a voluntary parent-run group or a privately run playgroup.

Parent and toddler groups

These are also voluntary, non-profit making and usually make a small charge. They are for mothers, sometimes fathers or carers of children under three where babies and toddlers can get together and have a good time. The parent or carer must stay with the child.

These are run by voluntary community groups, amenity groups or perhaps the community play service. The borough Social Services Department would have a list.

Cost: Voluntary donation.

Maternity leave: the law

Women are now protected in their jobs and cannot be fired for becoming pregnant. However, your announcement that you are pregnant will be greeted differently, depending on your position in the company, your expendability, the sort of crisis any absence on your part creates, and how the people you work with and for relate to you personally. If you are indispensable to the running of your company, you can hardly blame your boss for reacting to the news with some distress. If you have been talking about having a baby for years, and it finally happens, there will, no doubt, be congratulations all round.

The Maternity Alliance produces a book called *Women, Work and Maternity,* describing women's experiences of being pregnant at their place of work, taking maternity leave and returning to work. The experiences vary considerably from the positive to the negative. Some complaints were justified and some a little far-fetched. Whether you are able to sympathise with the unmarried teacher at the Catholic school who was caused terrible stress by the head teacher's threats, based on his own and the school governors' disapproval of her pregnancy, that she might lose her job, depends on your religion, your politics and your sense of humour.

Returning to work after the baby is born can be made very stressful, as everyone, and particularly all women, has views on what a mother's role should be in relation to her new baby. Colleagues in your place of work will not hesitate to express them. Listen, and then do what you believe is right.

Your employer should inform you about your statutory entitlement to maternity pay and leave. Your trade union, Citizens' Advice Bureau (CAB) and local clinic will have the information you need. Never go to a CAB without telephoning first for times of opening. Don't try to phone during office hours, ie 9–5, as you can hang on for half an hour without the phone being answered. The offices all have telephone answering machines which give you the times of opening. Telephone very early in the morning or in the evening for the recorded information. CABs are manned by voluntary staff and are never open all day, every day of the week.

The relevant leaflets from the DSS are: N1 257 Employer's Guide to Statutory Maternity Pay; N1 17A Maternity Benefits. They are supposed to be available from your local social security offices but are often out of stock. If you write to: DSS Leaflets, PO Box 21, Stanmore, Middlesex HA7 1AY and wait patiently, you should receive them by and by.

Booklet No 4, *Employment Rights for the Expectant Mother* from the Department of Employment tells you about your rights in your place of employment.

Nanny agencies report a high rate of cancellation by mothers who hire a nanny with every intention of returning to work, and then find they cannot bear to part with their baby. The degree of scepticism with which your employer greets your commitment to return after the baby is born depends entirely on your commitment to your job, your relationship with him, and his previous experience. There may be no doubt whatsoever that you will return to work as soon as possible. On the other hand, your employer may be biding his time, waiting for actions to speak louder than words. It is up to you to be totally honest and straightforward with your employer as to your intentions, as soon as you know yourself what they are.

The experience of many mothers, both from employers' observation and from their own experience, is that returning to work after the second baby is born is more difficult, particularly for women who have not developed a reliable support system. If this is in the form of live-in childcare, the arrival of the second child presents fewer problems than the first as the adjustments have already been made. However, having to surmount the complications of taking little children of varying ages to different kinds of carers every day leads many mothers, by the time the third baby is born, to opt for a career break.

How much time off you are allowed

You are allowed paid time off for ante-natal care. You may be asked by your employer, after the first visit, to show proof that you are pregnant in the form of a certificate from your doctor or health visitor and your appointment card verifying your appointment dates.

Women have the statutory right to 11 weeks off work before the due date for the baby. You must return to work no later than 29 weeks after the baby is born to get the same terms and conditions of employment. Since 1980 your company has not been obliged to give you exactly the same job back, but the terms and conditions must be equal to the one you left.

If it is either impossible or illegal for you to do your job while pregnant, the employer must offer alternative employment. If there is no alternative employment, you do not lose your right either to Statutory Maternity Pay or to return to work after maternity absence.

Companies with fewer than five employees don't have to reinstate a woman employee if it's not 'reasonably practicable'.

To qualify for statutory maternity leave, you have to have worked for the same company continuously for more than 16 hours a week for two years up to the time of maternity leave (11 weeks before the due date). If you work between 8 and 16 hours a week, you must have worked for five years continuously for the same company up to 11 weeks before the due date.

Everything must be in writing

At least 21 days before beginning maternity leave, you must inform your employer in writing that you are leaving work to have a baby, what your expected week of confinement is and that you intend to return to work after the baby is born.

After you have left to start your maternity leave, your employer has the right to be informed in writing whether you intend to return. Your employer will ask you by post, no earlier than 49 days after the start of the expected week of confinement, to let him know in writing if you intend to return to work. You must reply within *14 days* of receiving the letter or you lose your right to return.

Write to your employer within 14 days of receiving the above letter telling him that you intend to return to work. Write to your employer again *not later than 21 days before you intend to return* informing him of the exact date of your return.

Statutory Maternity Pay (SMP)

SMP is taxable and subject to National Insurance contributions. It is payable for a period of 18 weeks in total, the first 6 weeks at a higher rate if you have worked either 16 hours a week or more for the same employer for over two years, or 8–16 hours a week for the same employer for five years. In that case you are paid 90 per cent of your salary for six weeks. This is calculated on your earnings for eight weeks up to the qualifying week. For the following 12 weeks, everybody gets the same amount of £36.25 per week.

If your baby is premature, maternity pay starts the week after the baby is born.

What if you haven't worked for two years for the same employer?

You receive the lower rate of £36.25 per week for the full 18-week maternity period, provided you have worked for 26 hours a week up to 15 weeks prior to the due date.

Who pays you SMP?

The employer now pays the employee directly. The employer then deducts what he has paid plus 7½ per cent from his monthly payments to the Inland Revenue. The 7½ per cent covers the employer's costs in bookkeeping and clerical work to do the work formerly done by the DHSS. It works in exactly the same way as Statutory Sick Pay (SSP).

What if you don't qualify for SMP at all?

You are entitled to *maternity allowance* when you have reached the fourteenth week prior to the week the baby is due. Unlike SMP, there is no tax or National Insurance contributions on maternity allowance. It is paid for 18 weeks. If you do not qualify for maternity allowance, your claim will automatically be considered for sickness benefit. Your maternity certificate is accepted as evidence of incapacity for work for the period starting six weeks before the week the baby is due to 14 days after the date on which the baby is born.

The DSS leaflets are: MA 1 Maternity Allowance and NI 16 Sickness Benefit. Both are available from your social security office or health clinic.

In and out of the money!

You are allowed 40 weeks in total away from your job, 11 weeks before the baby is born and 29 weeks after. You are paid SMP for 18 of those which leaves 22 unsalaried weeks. For whatever reason, if you have need of supplementary income, you can apply for *family credit*.

Family credit replaced family income supplement in April 1989. It is a regular weekly tax-free non-contributory payment to working people who are responsible for at least one child under the age of 16 (or 19 if in full-time education). You don't need to have paid NICs (National Insurance contributions) to qualify. Family credit is an *income-related* benefit whereby the amount of family credit you receive depends on your or your partner's earnings and savings. Your social security office will be able to tell you about it.

The information is in DSS booklet NI 261 A Guide to Family Credit.

Real financial need

Mothers who need extra cash help to provide necessities for the new baby can apply for an extra payment from the Social Fund. You apply for a maternity payment from the Social Fund by obtaining a claim form from your social security office. You can apply any time from 11 weeks before the baby is due until it is three months old. The payment is £85 for each baby expected, (you might find you have real financial need if you have twins or triplets), but the total amount will be reduced by any savings over £500 that you and your partner have.

Company childcare schemes

Women have always shown, in surveys of what attracts people to what jobs, that they are more concerned about liking their job than about the size of the weekly pay cheque and the promise of perks. There is, however, one perk for women, more powerful in its attraction than any other, that will be instrumental in winning or losing the loyalty of female employees, and that is help with childcare.

The workplace nursery is dealt with thoroughly in Chapter 4. The Midland Bank has announced that by 1993 it hopes to have 300 workplace nurseries in operation, either on its own or with co-operation from other companies or local authorities.

Topping up maternity pay is another inducement. Royal UK, a subsidiary of Royal Insurance, is offering returning new mothers, who would previously only have been entitled to the statutory six weeks' SMP at 90 per cent of their salary, an extra two months' bonus paid six months after they return to work, based on their salary at the time of payment. Their cheap home loan rates – the subsidised mortgage they lose on giving up work to have children – will be repaid in a lump sum in their first month's salary after re-employment. Royal's deal, agreed with the Manufacturing, Science and Finance Union will give women employees help with their mortgages and cash handouts of up to £2000.

Luncheon Vouchers Ltd expects to launch its *Childcare Vouchers* by September 1989. The vouchers will be exchangeable for childcare only, be it a nursery, a nanny, a minder or even a relative. There will be a small service charge to the company and a minimal administration charge to the carer. The employer will determine the value of the vouchers and who will be eligible. The benefit of the voucher scheme to the employee is that, because they are not exchangeable for cash, they are free from National Insurance for both the company and the employee.

At the end of a job interview, expect to be told not only about pension rights, health insurance programmes and holiday allowance, but also what the company is doing about childcare provision. If you are not told, *ask*.

Unfortunately, all the above schemes are considered to be part of the recipient's income and are taxed with the rest of income as any so-called 'perk' would be.

Foundations, societies and voluntary organisations

Some organisations are mentioned where appropriate in the text. Others are described below.

The Working Mothers Association
77 Holloway Road, London N7 8JZ; 01-700 5771

This organisation started because working mothers in Clapham who had got together through the National Childbirth Trust wanted to set up a mutual support group. They produced *The Working Mothers Handbook* based on their own experiences. The *Handbook* produced such a demand for similar groups that in 1985 they formed nationally into the Working Mothers Association for the purpose of helping future working mothers by providing local support groups and information and advice regarding every aspect of a working mother's life. The great strength of the Working Mothers Association is the local groups. There are 70 so far around the country, all started as self-help organisations by local, enthusiastic working parents.

When you join you are put in touch with your local group; if there isn't one you are offered help in setting up a group. As well as offering help and advice to mothers regarding childcare, the value of networking and mututal support, the Association works towards better childcare provision by providing information and working with policy-makers and employers for the welfare of working mothers with children.

The groups provide a social context for working mothers to share experiences and give advice on childcare. Many groups have put together lists of local childcare agencies and nursery schools with their current rates. This is a marvellous opportunity for useful networking by local mothers. They can provide mutual assistance in solving not only the problems of childcare and every organisational dilemma facing a working mother but also a forum for discussing the emotional problems of guilt and worry.

The National Childcare Campaign (NCCC)
Wesley House, 4 Wild Court, London WC2B 5AU; 01-405 5617

From their own information: 'NCCC is a voluntary organisation, set up in 1980, which supports and is supported by parents, childcare professionals and others concerned with providing flexible child-care facilities in the UK. We are a national membership organisation and provide a platform both nationally and locally to promote childcare issues.'

The Daycare Trust (DCT)
Wesley House, 4 Wild Court, London WC2B 5AU; 01-405 5617

From their own information: 'The Daycare Trust – a charity set up in 1986 – is a sister organisation to the National Childcare Campaign. We provide a hotline service to deal with thousands of enquiries from parents, educationists and childcare workers who need information about where childcare is to be found, how to improve it and how to go about setting up a project. We deal with calls from individuals, local authority officers and the voluntary sector, as well as employers and employees in the private sector.'

Gingerbread
35 Wellington Street, London WC2E 7BN; 01-240 0953

For lone parents and children, Gingerbread provides support for one-parent families by providing advice on legal, financial and social problems as well as advising parents on how to network for self-help. If you write to them they will send you a list of their helpful publications ranging from Gingerbread's *Social Policy Statement*, to *Starting a Crèche*, to *Holiday Guide for One-Parent Families*.

The Thomas Coram Foundation for Children
Head Office: 41 Brunswick Square, London WC1N 1AZ; 01-278 2424

The Coram Children's Centre provides nursery care and services to under-fives and their families; the Adoption Service strives to place children with special needs in adoptive families; the 529 Project helps young people bridge the gap between adolescence and adulthood by providing residential help and care and non-residential group activities; the Meeting Place provides a safe and confidential venue for parents and children in need; and the Homeless Children's Project help for parents and children without accommodation.

The National Council for One Parent Families (NCOPF)
255 Kentish Town Road, London NW5 2LX; 01-267 1361

This is a charity and the service is free and confidential. The service includes advice on legal and taxation problems, housing problems, social security and maintenance, and pregnancy counselling. Enquiries are dealt with nationally by phone and letter and, where appropriate, parents are put in touch with local organisations or individuals who can help. One Parent Families' advisers also represent lone parents at appeal tribunals and the advice department provides training on legal and welfare rights for one-parent family groups and for professionals on specific issues affecting one-parent families.

Husbands and fathers

Endless articles promoting participation and sharing by husbands in running the household conclude that there has been a marked difference in input in the last few years. Unfortunately, this is rarely borne out in studies of the current role of fathers, particularly after divorce. Every survey on this subject comes to a different conclusion, probably more accurately reflecting the wishful thinking and foregone conclusions of the folk doing the survey than the reality.

Few men, it seems, unless abandoned to run the whole show themselves, have any idea of how much work is actually involved.

I have even heard of mothers who have deserted the nest on Friday night leaving the children, a temporary baby-sitter with instructions to leave the minute the husband arrives home, and a note, 'Gone for the weekend, darling. I need a break and have to get away. I know you won't mind. See you Monday morning', signed, 'Your loving wife.' For the full effect, it is essential to forewarn all your friends and relatives, whom he might call on in desperation, to be too busy to lend a hand. After a weekend of single parenting, some fathers' attitudes have changed overnight, as it were.

'Observe the fathers in the playground on Sunday morning and they are usually reading the Sunday papers and talking to each other while the children get on with playing with each other.' This is Charlie Lewis's observation in *Becoming a Father*.[2] 'There is a huge variety of experiences of fatherhood, from the man who inseminates a woman after a disco and doesn't even know he is a father, to the male single parent who gives up his job to look after his children full time. In between is the vast majority who do what they can within constraints but do much less than their wives.'

Since it is the woman who has the baby, most women feel that it is their responsibility to juggle baby, home and job and keep things running smoothly.

Most men are over the moon at the thought of becoming a father but are confused about the commitment that must come subsequently. After a career break, when a mother decides to return to work, her husband may welcome the concept of a second income but then fail to contribute to the domestic chores. Many husbands were reported as having given lip-service to feminism and the women's movement but, when it came to putting their words into action, it was a different story. There is little evidence to suggest that fathers help more with the routine, repetitive household chores. Unhappily, 'Some men grant approval to their wives working as long as it has no effect on family life.'[3] Women often collude with this attitude, insisting constantly that their husband's work doesn't suffer and their children don't suffer because of their jobs. There were some husbands who were paragons of help among the mothers I interviewed. Not only did they help in the house, but sat on school committees or were parent governors of schools.

For lone mothers without the expectation of help from a husband, life can be a real struggle. The number of one-parent families has

2. Open University Press, 1986, from Maternity Alliance Charter.
3. *Double Identity*, Sue Sharpe, page 176.

doubled in the last 17 years.[4] Only 50 per cent of men pay most of the agreed maintenance most of the time. Six months after divorce only 50 per cent of men keep in contact with their children.[5] This may be more from lack of being able to cope with the new relationship and the children's confusion. There is a big difference between being the warm body, securely available in the next room, and approaching one's own children like a kindly uncle taking them out for a Sunday treat. This is very difficult for all parties concerned, especially the mother who has done all the disciplining, organising and complaining about the untidy bedrooms all week, and who finds 'Daddy bountiful' standing at the door on Sunday. Also if the marriage has broken up because of a father's new relationship, there are other demands on his time at the weekend.

Communicate before you move the goalposts

First check to see that your husband's communication dial is on 'receive' not 'send'. With a lot of men, it is locked permanently into the 'send' position and very hard to budge.

Your husband may not have understood your intention to stay in your job after the baby is born, your expectation of his sharing the household tasks, and the realigning of chores and responsibilities.

Most women nowadays don't have a real option of giving up work to take care of the family, but no man has that option. Studies in America of professional couples have shown that there can be some degree of resentment on the part of a husband whose wife feels she always has the option open to her to give up the rat-race and retire, as a full-time mother, to the pastoral calm of the suburbs with the children.

Building a career is hard, work is hard, and the end of the day can leave your husband in a state of absolute exhaustion too. It is not reasonable to present him with a redesigned life-style where he feels he has had no say in the matter. A husband may not want to participate in decisions very much and may be relieved to be able to off-load all the domestic matters on his wife but, if he does want to be involved, his feelings and opinions should not be ignored. If he thinks he doesn't want to be involved in the decision-making, he should, at least, be kept informed of what decisions have been made.

4. 'Proposal for a Council Directive on Parental Leave and Leave for Family Reasons: Background Paper (unpublished), P. Moss, 11 July 1984.
5. Information from *Sunday Times* article, 26 February 1989, Dorothy Wade quoting Mavis Maclean from Oxford University's Centre for Socio-Legal Studies.

The invisible contract

You have probably never heard of the invisible contract. Most mothers only dimly begin to remember its existence two or three years after the birth of their first baby, being too euphoric after the birth of baby number one, either from the sheer joy of achievement after the delivery or perhaps the laughing gas, to remember signing on the dotted line. My own memory is fairly hazy too, but I know for sure that I signed it. It is brought to you by a kind of angel, the patron saint of mothers, just after the baby is born. It reads something like this:

I, _____(Your name)_____, do hereby promise from this day

forth _____(the date)_____ to undertake the following:

> I will never need a full night's sleep again.
> I will never be tired again.
> I will never be sick again.
> I will never be irritable again.
> I will never lose my temper again.
> I will never be alone again.

The final one is the most important and this you must remember for always. Once you have a baby, you *have* a baby, for life! There are only a very few places after you become a mother where you can ever hope to be completely alone. You will find that children have no compunctions about holding long conversations from the other side of the toilet door. One of the best places to nail a mother as a captive audience is while she is in the bath.

There is one fail-safe way of being alone I know of, but it helps here to be Catholic. On your knees, holding a missal and crucifix, making your way slowly up the steps and across the courtyard to the altar of your cathedral, no one would dare intrude. Don't ever mock those pious women for their devotion. Not only is it very real, but the hour they spend on their knees is probably the only form of peace and rest they ever get.

Chapter 2

Your Job

Your rights in your job

Once you have decided to start a family, or are already holding the baby for that matter, only you can decide how you want to proceed with your job. Only you can decide how and whether you are going to combine fulfilling career ambitions with fulfilment as a mother and a wife. The decision you come to must be based on your own understanding of yourself, your needs, your husband's and family's needs, and your capabilities.

It will be a compromise. All decisions of this nature are a compromise. Make sure it provides the greatest amount of happiness, for most of you, most of the time.

Businesses sympathetic to the conflicts of responsibilities and obligations in a new mother's life are accepting that a talented woman will want to step, temporarily, out of the fast lane, in order to balance her job with her family. Putting temporary limitations on the growth of a career because of family responsibilities doesn't mean you have given up all those hopes and dreams; it just means they are simmering on a back burner until a time when you can get back on the career ladder when the family responsibilities lessen.

You are not trying to achieve a fair deal for yourself in a vacuum. The Equal Opportunities Commission, the Training Agency and the European Community agencies have been set up to protect your rights.

The Equal Opportunities Commission was established by Parliament to ensure effective enforcement of the Sex Discrimination Acts of 1975 and 1986 – and the Equal Pay Act. One important function of the Commission is to advise you of your rights under these Acts – rights which could have an effect on your career prospects as well as your pay packet. The Sex Discrimination Acts make it unlawful to treat anyone, on the ground of sex, less favourably than a person of the opposite sex is or would be treated in the same circumstances. Women at work can now be secure in the knowledge that they have the legal right not to be harassed, molested or in any way bothered by uninvited, unprovoked and unwanted overt sexual attention. In employment, and some other limited circumstances, it is also unlawful to discriminate against married people. The EOC exists to help *you*. It is there to fight for your rights: in what you are paid, in your career prospects, even in your chances of getting a mortgage. It has a library and comprehensive information service. *Use it.*

The Equal Opportunities Commission
England: Manchester *Headquarters*
             Overseas House, Quay Street, Manchester M3 3HN;
             061-833 9244

Scotland: Glasgow *Scottish Regional Office*
             St Andrew House, 141 West Nile Street, Glasgow G1
             2RN; 041-332 8018

Wales: Cardiff *Welsh Regional Office*
             Caerwys House,   Windsor Lane,   Cardiff CF1 1LB;
             0222 343552

Hours of work for women

According to the Employment Act of 1989, women are now entitled to work the same hours as men. The only exceptions, which apply equally to both sexes, are where there is a risk to health and safety.

Don't retire to a corner and sulk if you feel you have been discriminated against or treated unfairly because you have family obligations, are pregnant, have taken a career break or are much older than the other candidates.

New ways to work

New Ways to Work is an independent organisation which aims through education and research to advance knowledge about all aspects of flexible working patterns. It promotes new approaches to the time patterns of paid work to encourage equal access to jobs for people who have caring and domestic responsibilities and for anyone unable or unwilling to fit into traditional work patterns.

It runs a Job Share Partner Register for the London area using a computerised database which matches people according to the type of work they wish to do and the area of London they wish to work in. It advises and gives information to individuals as well as acting as consultant to companies on how to redescribe jobs to turn them into job shares.

New Ways to Work
309 Upper Street, London N1 2TV; 01-226 4026

Job sharing

Job sharing is a way of working where two or more people share one full-time job between them. Each sharer does half the work, and receives half the pay, holidays and other benefits of the job, including in some cases pension rights. Since April 1987 local government employees working more than 15 but less than 30 hours a week qualify for the pension scheme. The benefits to the sharer are enormous; unlike a part-time job, which usually has neither status nor future, job sharing allows qualified people with restrictions on their time, for whatever reason, to keep a foot firmly on the professional ladder, keep abreast of developments in their field of expertise, and retain a permanent relationship with a company.

It is likely that job sharing will overtake flexitime as the solution to retaining a high standard while giving people the freedom to work the hours permitted by their other responsibilities. This applies not only to mothers with young children, but to men and women responsible for elderly or disabled relatives, people nearing retirement who wish to slow down but not stop altogether and people with skills to offer who haven't 40 hours a week to spare.

There is much more job sharing in the public sector than in the private sector so far. However, the private sector, recognising the skill saving and economic advantage, is coming round to the idea.

British Telecom runs a job sharing scheme that covers 200,000 employees and may be the largest in Britain. The move has come about because BT is aware that the drop in school-leavers will leave them with skill shortages unless they nurture the skills already available to them. BT promises that it will make reasonable efforts to accommodate job sharing and that job sharers will be treated in accordance with BT rules as far as promotion, pay, conditions of employment, maternity pay and leave, and superannuation entitlements are concerned.

Part-time work

This is the least attractive of all the options. A woman who returns to part-time work after having a baby usually does so in a capacity that under-exploits her skills. Eighty-five per cent of Britain's four million part-time workers are women.[1] The Department of Employment survey, *Women and Employment*, found that 45 per cent of the women who had returned to part-time work were in a job of a lower occupational category than their last job before having children.[2] One must have a particularly enlightened, sympathetic and creative company to find ways of really using women's skills on a part-time basis. However, it may be that the demands of running a home and family are such that for a short period, an undemanding, fairly stressless part-time job is more suitable. Currently, one woman in six works less than 16 hours a week.[3] Job sharing, which allows you to use your skills part time, is a better option, but both sorts of employment are hard to find.

Career breaks

These can come under the description of re-entry or reservist schemes. The company is not under an obligation to rehire the individual but places individuals on a reserve list and considers them for suitable vacancies at the same level at which they left the company. The National Westminster Bank introduced such a scheme in 1981 to male and female staff to enable them to take an extended break of up to five years for childcare. Those selected must agree to work for a minimum of two weeks a year and attend an annual one-day seminar. They are kept up to date with information packs and company information. Other banks have introduced similar schemes. British Gas has a scheme called the Skills Retention Scheme. Employers featured in a recent study tended to be banks, government (nationalised) companies or the Civil Service.

During a career break, the company should keep employees abreast of changes and developments by sending them company literature and magazines and inviting them to company events.

Hatfield Polytechnic has been awarded funding from the government's Training Agency for two Professional Updating courses. The course is nine weeks long and is aimed at giving women confidence to re-enter the labour market after a career break by familiarising them with new legislation, current market behaviour and business finance. The course has been going since

1. *Practical Approaches to Women's Career Development*, Cooper (ed), Manpower Services Commission, 1983.
2. *The Employer's Guide to Childcare*, Working Mothers Association.
3. *Women and Employment: A Lifetime Perspective*, J Martin and C Roberts, Department of Employment.

1988. By 1990 there will be similar courses at Manchester Polytechnic, Trent Polytechnic in Nottingham, Humberside College of Higher Education in Hull and the University of Exeter. The places are limited to women who have a profession, although not necessarily a degree, and have a serious intention of re-entering their profession. Women participating are assigned an academic supervisor in their own field so that they get tuition and updating in that specific field. One day each week and one full work week is spent in a placement.

This sort of course is ideal for a woman who has taken a prolonged career break and no longer has contact with her former employer. If you left your job before the concept of a career break was a possibility, here is your chance to design your own. Depending on your academic tutor, you should receive direct help in finding employment in your field and you would certainly find yourself linking up with your profession again. The only disadvantage to the career break is that it can serve to polarise the domestic chores between the husband and wife. You may have to retrain your husband once you return to your job.

Flexitime

The hours we work are based more on tradition than on people's domestic obligations and changing needs. Nine to five, Monday to Friday, with an hour for lunch is an outdated concept. If everyone works the same hours, everyone travels to work at the same time and comes home at the same time and in the most disagreeable conditions. If everyone has the same two days off in the week, leisure pursuits are oversubscribed, crowded and not an attractive prospect. There is, in many instances, no need to confine staff to traditional working hours when with a little imagination and leeway mothers would be allowed the time to deliver children to school in the morning or collect them in the afternoon and spend more time with them. A husband and wife, both of whom are on flexitime, can make arrangements much more easily so that all their mutual responsibilities are covered than parents who must comply with traditional hours of working.

A company that institutes flexitime stipulates the number of hours everyone must work and also the core hours during which everyone is obliged to be *at* work. For example, the core hours might be from 10 am to 4.30 pm. Employees then may be allowed to start as early as 8 or finish as late as 7 provided they work an eight-hour day including the core hours.

Evening and night work

Doctors, nurses, teachers, office cleaners – there are all sorts of jobs that can be done in the evening or at night. Many women without skills or training take work in the evening or at night because it fits in with the sharing of childcare with their husbands and brings in extra money. Seventy-eight per cent of all evening workers are mothers of dependent children.[4] Women do it because they need the extra money, but it is not easy and is very hard on the marital relationship. Working nights and sleeping days is also very hard on the system and cannot be kept up for ever, but the reward is the extra income that working unsocial hours brings.

Working from home

This is becoming more and more common and there are many sorts of professional work that are portable, from computers to engineering. The company provides the equipment, be it computers or drawing boards, and the women, with a phone and contact to the office, can complete part of their job if not all of it from a home base. The disadvantage is that rather than retain full-time employment, you tend to work mega-full time. If your office is at home you can find yourself working on Saturday, Sunday and at 3 o'clock in the morning. The company finds it is getting more than good value for what it is paying and you find that you are working longer hours and harder than when you went into the office from 9 to 5. Work at home doesn't start and stop at given times. It goes on for ever. There is also the tendency not to count any time at home as work unless you are crouched over the desk. At the office, you would accept the need for coffee breaks, a sensible lunch break, and intervals of mental relaxation, a joke with a passing colleague. At home there is none of that, and you might find that you treat yourself very hard.

The computer industry is keen for women to continue part-time work at home. Because the industry moves and changes so fast, it is the only way that women on maternity leave or taking a break to have a baby can keep up. FI Group Plc, a computer company founded in 1962, has a 90 per cent female workforce. A large percentage work from home, while others work at client sites. The company provides work centres where employees can come to talk to other members of a team. As yet they are not providing crèche facilities. People working entirely from home would be working freelance and they include men as well as women. Employees have

4. *Women and Employment. See note 2 on page 36.*

an overall productivity rate of over 90 per cent. The earnings, paid by the hour, are highly competitive. Employees must work a minimum of 20 hours a week but, of course, the hours are flexible and with a computer line someone in the north of Scotland can be working on a project for south-east England.

This sort of work is convenient for a working mother. There is no wasted time and energy, as the travelling time is limited to the distance from your kitchen to your computer. The pay is hourly. A contract programmer would earn much more. Contact FI Group Plc, Chesham House, Church Lane, Berkhamsted, Hertfordshire; 0442 875051.

The drawback to this kind of employment is the isolation. Adult company providing mental stimulation is a powerful human need. Working from home requires a great deal of self-discipline and can be very lonely. There is also no job security and no sick pay. You are only paid for the time you work.

Freelance

Freelance work exists in many areas. You have to establish yourself in the profession first and you are only as good as your last job. If you are very good, you can find yourself working as many hours as when you were in full-time employment. Researchers for the advertising industry or the media, teachers, producers, editors, writers; the list of professions that can be pursued on a freelance basis is endless. Many women have a large portfolio of skills that they can draw on for different kinds of work. Women are far ahead of men on this if they have taken a career break to have a family and have found they can apply their skills in all kinds of areas.

Starting your own business

Few women entrepreneurs start businesses in manufacturing. The majority offer services often related to their own domestic experience. Women entrepreneurs with families display tremendous energy and ingenuity as, unlike their male counterparts who often rely on the unpaid back-up and work of their wives, the women go it alone, shouldering the domestic burden at the same time. For entrepreneurial men, the benefits of the unpaid labour of their wives is essential for a successful start-up to business. Entrepreneurial women often see marriage as a hindrance to success. Among managerial and professional women there is a lower rate of

39

marriage than among females as a whole.[5] Where husbands often do help out is in financial back-up, removing the initial element of risk.

Women starting their own businesses often deliberately keep the business small, despite its success and natural growth, because they feel they cannot personally control a large organisation and they lack the personnel skills needed to employ people. The first thing you have to decide is the nature of your business and how you perceive its growth.

In starting up their own business, married women enjoy the advantage of having the financial security of their husband's income during the start-up period. The disadvantage they must deal with is that they cannot concentrate wholly and exclusively on the business, off-loading their domestic responsibilities on to a 'wife', and they can't exploit the free labour of a 'wife' to do all the dogsbody chores while they get on with exercising their entrepreneurial flair.

Many women run home-based businesses, not anticipating growth and concentrating on service areas encompassing a traditional role such as cooking, dressmaking or hairdressing. It is usually not very profitable, nor is it expected to be, providing little more than pin-money but on a steady basis. The woman whose business it is would consider it very much secondary to her domestic responsibilities. Little enterprises can grow despite themselves, however, whereupon the proprietor has to assume a more professional approach.

The professional woman, using her skills to manage a small, home-based business where she anticipates growth and new customers, has to put her business responsibilities on an equal footing with her domestic ones. When push comes to shove, in order to retain the customers, the business must take priority. However, it is considerably more comfortable and convenient to work until four in the morning at home than in an office. Often this sort of business starts as a professional freelance career in areas such as advertising, market research or public relations.

You have to decide what sort of business you are going to start, whether you want to be innovative and dedicate yourself to growth, or whether you want to control a cosy little business that is profitable but controllable. Trading from home allows you to use equipment for both domestic and business purposes and account for these in

5. *Women in Charge: The Experience of Female Entrepreneurs*, Gaffee and Scase, George Allen & Unwin 1985.

the most efficient way for tax purposes.

A selection of books for those starting up or running a business is published by Kogan Page.

Chapter 3

Who is Qualified to Take Care of Your Children?

The qualifications that represent training and competence in childcare are not mandatory requirements in getting a job. Local authorities say that all nurseries must have a certain proportion of trained staff but, while writing this book, I visited nurseries where none of the staff had a formal qualification. They were lovely people with loads of experience, but without formal qualifications of any kind. In residential work, any girl can call herself a nanny from day one in the job with no training or experience whatsoever.

Here is what the government is doing about it: the National Council for Vocational Qualifications (NCVQ), set up in 1986, is attempting to co-ordinate all the various nursery and day-care qualifications. The government has also set up the Care Sector Consortium concerned with the care sector of work covering health care, workers in local government employ, residential homes, the voluntary sector and in the private sector which would include nannies.

National Council for Vocational Qualifications
222 Euston Road, London NW1 2BZ; 01-387 9898

To NNEB or not to NNEB
In residential work, anyone can call themselves a nanny and get away with it. 'Nanny' is not a professional title like Doctor or Lieutenant.

It isn't only the girls who abuse the term. Calling your mother's help or minder 'the nanny' has a nice ring of money about it, and many employers indulge in poetic licence when referring to their childcarer.

Besides, some employers don't want a girl who is too thoroughly trained because they think she won't be malleable enough. They don't want a dictatorial, starched, old-fashioned nanny in the house. An untrained girl is also cheaper.

However, no one can put the letters NNEB after her name unless she has done the course. Heads of nurseries certainly need to have an NNEB as a minimum qualification, as do a proportion of the staff. A girl who has done two or even three years on an NNEB course is showing a good degree of tenacity and dedication before she has been interviewed by you. The content of the NNEB course is very thorough and the girl who has done it is a professional.

Whether you are employing a nanny with NNEB training or not, or putting your child in day care, you should know what it means. To find out what sort of training the NNEB qualification provides, send for the National Nursery Examination Board booklet (£1) which is an up-to-date overview of what the course entails.

The National Nursery Examination Board
8 Chequer Street, St Albans, Hertfordshire AL1 3XZ; 0727 47636 or 67333

As well as the famous fee-paying private nursery nurse residential colleges, Norlands, the Princess Christian, and the Chiltern Nursery Training College, there are over 170 colleges throughout Britain and approved centres overseas offering two-year courses leading to the Certificate in Nursery Nursing. The Board will also supply an up-to-date list of these colleges.

The Board's Certificate is nationally recognised for employment purposes in England, Wales and Northern Ireland. The Scottish Nursery Nurses' Board offers a similar qualification.

The Board also offers a Certificate in Post Qualifying Studies for people who want to take more specialist advanced study.

The NNEB syllabus is all-encompassing, covering all areas of the child's development from birth to the age of seven. I recommend the *Overview* as required reading for any parent who has a blasé attitude to child-rearing. It is an edifying document which should definitely make you take your role as a parent more seriously.

There are only three residential nursery training establishments in Britain:

The Princess Christian Nursery Training College
26 Wilbraham Road, Fallowfield, Manchester M14 6JX; 061-224 4560

Entry requirements
Minimum age: 17½

Academic qualifications: three GCSEs, A B or C grade including English

Course length: two years, intake in January and September

Qualifications gained: Students receive Certificates of the NNEB and the Royal Society of Health as well as the Princess Christian Certificate.

Employment: The college maintains a list of prospective employers and for the first two years monitors every nurse's progress offering advice and support.

Practical training: This is available both inside the college in their own day-care unit and in nearby teaching hospitals, in local authority nursery and infant schools and in a nursery school integrating children with special needs. A residential placement is included in the second year.

Norland Nursery Training College Ltd
Denford Park, Hungerford, Berkshire RG17 0PQ; 0488 82252

Entry requirements
Minimum age: 18

Academic qualifications: three GCSE passes at A B or C grades; one must be English

Course length: two years, intake January and September

Qualifications gained: Certificate of the NNEB and the Royal Society of Health Diploma of Nursery Nursing; Norland Diploma and Badge gained after nine months' work as a Probationer Nurse in a private residential post arranged through the Norland Registry.

Employment: The college keeps a register of comprehensive files on all Norland nurses together with detailed records of potential employers and matches these with the help of a computer.

Practical training: The school itself, Denford Park, has a lavishly equipped day nursery and a residential nursery which accommodates 22 children.

Chiltern Nursery Training College
16 Peppard Road, Caversham, Reading RG4 8JZ; 0734 471847

Entry requirements
Minimum age: 18

Academic qualifications: O level or equivalent passes in at least three subjects, one of which should be English

Course length: two years, intake in January and September

Qualifications gained: Royal Society of Health Diploma in Nursery Nursing and the NNEB Certificate.

Employment: The school does not keep a register or help its graduates to find jobs.

Practical training: Students spend approximately six months of the course in each of the college day nurseries with babies and children aged 0–2 and 0–5. One term is spent in a nursery school, either the college's own or a local state nursery; half a term in a local primary school; eight weeks in a maternity department and eight weeks working with either sick children or those with special needs.

A Norlands or Princess Christian nanny will, more often than not, go back to college when looking for a new job, but because they are so highly in demand, word of mouth is also an effective way of finding a job. Glamour jobs with famous people will usually go through the college or an agency. A famous client is usually not identified by the school or the agency until the girl has been approved.

Courses for childminders are described in Chapter 5.

Chapter 4

Day-Care Options

Full-time care

Once you have decided that the best solution is for your child to attend a nursery, start researching what is available in your area and what the cost will be. Part-time or sessional nursery school will be of no use to you if you are in full-time employment and don't have help at home to cover the rest of the day.

Contact the Social Services Department of your local authority and ask them to send you lists of:

Registered private day nurseries
State nurseries and community nurseries
Registered playgroups
Parent and toddler groups
Nursery schools and classes

If you look in the Yellow Pages, you will find listings for Nurseries – Child and Nursery Schools with no differentiation between those offering all day care and those offering sessional or part-time care.

State and private all-day nurseries are open from around 8 am to 6 pm, 50 to 52 weeks of the year except for statutory holidays. They offer provision for children up to five years old, usually accepting babies at six months. Very few nursery schools will take babies younger than six months old, although there are nurseries which say they are open to children from 0 to 5. Some say they will accept a new-born baby and have nursing mothers coming in to feed the baby, but this is rare.

State and community all-day nurseries are heavily subsidised by the local authority. State nurseries are funded directly, while community nurseries usually receive grant aid. The lower fees are met in the former instance by the subsidy and in the latter by the grant. For example, in Aberdeen, single working mothers pay £8 per week for all-day state nursery care. The state subsidy amounts to about £93 per week, the real cost being £101 per child per week. In north London's Broadwater Farm area in Haringey, mothers with their children in a community nursery pay only £10 per week, the balance being covered by a local authority grant. Parents can pay as little as £5 per week for a child in a state nursery.

However, places in state nurseries are few and far between and are rarely available to the children of two-parent families. It isn't necessarily that the children who have access to state places are at risk or deprived, but that most Social Services Departments favour children who, in their view, have a real need of the place. These are the children of single parents, or parents on a low income where the extra stimulation of an all-day nursery place adds a measurable and essential dimension to a child's life. Research shows that children of single mothers benefit tremendously from the strong influence and presence of other adults in their lives besides their mothers who can't possibly be everything and everyone to their children.

Council day nurseries are supervised by the Social Services Department of the local authority. Private nurseries must be registered with the Social Services Department and are regularly inspected. It is unusual for under-five provision to be run by the Department of Education. However, Lothian and Strathclyde, the major regional authority in Scotland, have created their own under-fives unit which is managed by their Education Department.

You should know exactly how your own local authority functions and they should be happy to explain it to you. After all, you are paying for it.

The chance of getting your child a place

The chance of getting a place for your child in a council nursery is remote if he does not fit into their definition of a child with a special need for the place. Most local authorities report closed lists. This should not prevent you trying as the difference in cost is substantial but, unless you know you fulfil the requirements, it is advisable to turn your attention to privately run nurseries.

Waiting lists for private nurseries all over the country are long, usually at least a year. When a place becomes available, the nursery will call the families on their waiting list until they find someone who can take the place immediately. Local authorities told me that some nursery schools have simply had to close their lists. A nursery will usually give priority to a second child in a family so, once you have got your first child into a nursery, you can afford to relax a bit.

The cost of private nurseries varies little up and down the country. It is usually between £55 and £65 per week full time, but recently a number of new nurseries in business areas have opened as commercial enterprises charging over £100 per week.

The children are fed three meals a day, starting with breakfast as many children arrive with nothing more in their stomachs than a glass of juice. Lunch is a hot substantial meal followed by a lighter afternoon tea. In most nurseries, the parents must provide extras such as nappies, but there will be a laundry on the premises and everything else is provided.

If you send your child to a private nursery, you must expect to pay a lot more than you would if he was at a local authority-subsidised nursery. In fact, you must expect to pay the full market price for the facilities he enjoys there.

You may be fortunate enough to work in a place with a workplace nursery. So far these tend to be confined to hospitals, institutes of education and public services departments, and are heavily subsidised by the state.

Armed with every bit of information you can get through word of mouth, advice from your local clinic and health visitor, and information from the Day-Care Department of your local Social Services Department, and even the Yellow Pages, you must proceed like a general, fighting to the end, no holds barred, firmly fixed on your goal of finding a place for your child in a nursery.

For more information on what is available and should be available for the under-fives, contact the National Children's Bureau, 8 Wakley Street, London EC1V 7QE; 01-278 9441.

Sources of information

Voluntary Organisations Liaison Council for Under Fives (VOLCUF) 77 Holloway Road, London N7 8JZ; 01-607 9573

VOLCUF 'is a registered charity which aims to support and enhance the work of its members in promoting and developing improvements in services for children under five and their families. VOLCUF provides information and support, organises a programme of training, promotes good practice and acts as an advocate on behalf of the voluntary sector. VOLCUF has an equal opportunities policy and aims to develop and maintain links with black and other ethnic minority voluntary groups, and to promote anti-racist and anti-sexist childcare practice.'

Their leaflet, 'Daycare for Your Under-Fives', produced in association with the National Consumer Council provides a checklist and questions to ask when looking for suitable day care for your under-five. It tells you where to look, how to judge and what to expect. It also urges those who are not satisfied with the provision in their area to take action and tells you how.

Among its publications is 'Social Security Benefits for Families with a Young Child'. Published in December 1988, it is the only publication on welfare benefits to deal specifically with families with young children. It explains the differences between the old and new systems, and describes other benefits for families and also gives tables of benefit rates for 1988–89 and 1989–90.

Wandsworth Parents Information Centre
122 Plough Road, London SW11 2AL; 01-924 1391

The Wandsworth Parents Information Centre provides a service which is the first of its kind in the UK: a parents' information centre where free information and advice in seven languages (English, Bengali, Hindi, Urdu, Polish, French and Italian) on anything to do with children up to the age of 18 in the borough of Wandsworth is available. They will also advise anyone wishing to set up a similar service in their own borough.

The service is for parents seeking advice on any subject related to children, either for their children or for themselves; for example, a parent wanting to find out how to become a school governor.

The Information Centre has produced a booklet called *For Children* funded by a local department store, Arding and Hobbs. It is a directory for the children of working mothers in Wandsworth, extremely clearly set out with a wealth of information on every aspect of childcare.

There are already two non-profit making nurseries in Wandsworth. The cost is £1.70 per hour and they take babies from six weeks. The management of the day nurseries stresses that they are providing education with care.

Part-time care in nurseries and playgroups

There is an enormous variety of options available in sessional or part-time care. These can take the form of a Montessori or Rudolf Steiner nursery, a privately run nursery, nursery classes attached to a primary school, or a playgroup, either parent run or privately run. Mother and toddler groups, one o'clock clubs and the many varieties of drop-in centres welcome toddlers and even tinier children, accompanied by the person caring for them, for sessions up to three hours long.

Sessional care tends to be for older children, usually from 2½ or 3 to 5 year olds and breaks up for school holidays at Christmas, Easter and for the long summer break. This isn't much use to the working mother unless she has live-in childcare as the sessions cover only short periods of the day either in the morning or afternoon. Sessions are usually 2½ hours long lasting from 9.30 am to 12 and from 1 to 3.30 pm.

Nursery schools and classes

In the last few years, many local authorities have developed nursery education, either in the form of nursery schools or nursery classes as part of the infant school. Nursery children are always kept separate for play from the older children so they are not overwhelmed by football wielding seven-year-olds. Nursery class hours are part time, usually from 9 to 11.30 am and 1 to 3.30 pm. Although most places are part time, there are schools in some boroughs which are able to offer full-time places to some children. If your local infant school has no nursery classes, ask the Education Office about a place at another school close by.

Although there is nothing like adequate provision for the under-fives provided anywhere, research has shown conclusively that children who have some form of pre-school education do better subsequently. Nursery schools or classes attached to the primary school can provide the stimulation your child needs, the only drawback being that the classes are held in two short sessions and are thus not a provision for the child for the full extent of the parent's working day.

There are no regulations governing the size of a nursery school or playgroup but the building or space has to be adequate for the children. The Environmental Health Officer would advise on the maximum number of children allowable on inspecting the space. These nurseries are generally small, an ideal number being between 15 and 20 children with two to three adults.

The ratio of staff to child for sessional care is 1 to 8 and the head would be expected to have some sort of qualification. Empathy with the head is very important. Talk to her about her vision of what she is creating and the atmosphere in the school. The session should be disciplined and structured but an aura of kindness and gentleness should prevail.

The average cost for three hours a day in a small private nursery is about £300 per term. Some charge a little more and some a little less depending on the location, part of the country and length of the session. However, you should count on paying over £200 minimum per term.

Playgroups

These are usually non-profit making and require considerable commitment and involvement on the part of parents if parent run. Parents choose premises, form a committee of a chairman, secretary, and treasurer, hire play leaders and, with help and advice, run the group themselves. Note, though, that the playgroups do not have to be parent run. Playgroups, like all nurseries, must be registered. The Playgroup adviser or Organiser in your Social Services Department will advise parents on legal requirements and how to get a grant. The Pre-School Playgroups Association (PPA) offers advice and help, training courses for playgroup leaders in the form of foundation courses, short courses and further courses, and publishes a wide range of booklets and leaflets on every aspect of play, as well as two magazines, *Contact* and *Under Five*, for playgroups and parents of young children.

The PPA is a voluntary organisation linking playgroups and parent and toddler groups. It provides advice and information on setting up such groups, as well as practical help.

There are PPA offices all over the UK. Look in the telephone directory for the one near you. Only about 1 per cent of playgroups belonging to the PPA have hours appropriate for use by working parents.

Running Your Own Playgroup or Nursery by Jenny Willison (Kogan Page) is a practical guide for anyone who wants to set up and run their own playgroup or nursery.

Pre-School Playgroups Association
Head Office, 61–63 King's Cross Road, London WC1X 9LL;
01-833 0991

Parent and toddler groups

These are friendly meeting places where mothers, sometimes fathers, minders, nannies, au pairs or any carer can bring the baby or toddler, relax and enjoy the company of others while the baby does likewise. The carer cannot leave the child but is given the opportunity for a cup of tea and a chat while the baby plays with other babies and with toys and materials that are not available at home. Sessions are free, usually involving only a small contribution for refreshments. Parent and toddler groups are run by community play services or other voluntary community group and take place in schools, churches and local halls. As times and locations change constantly make sure your information is up to date by phoning your Social Services Department, Community Play Service. Parent and toddler groups have to be registered so they would be able to supply you with a list.

Looking at nursery schools

Very few nursery schools have been purpose built and it is unlikely that you will find an ideal structure with low windows and banks of toilets of varying sizes to suit every need. However, you should be aware of a basic format for the physical structure of the space and how it works for the children. A large and welcoming open space just inside the front door as an arrival point for children is a great plus. Nurseries in buildings not intended for children can often seem a rabbit warren of rooms joined by long dark corridors. Observe how much imagination has been employed to transform whatever the space was before into a nursery school.

The physical structure

Windows. Are the windows adult height or child height? If the nursery is in a house obviously the windows will be adult height, but in a purpose-built nursery they should be at child's eye level. There should also be observation windows or portholes between the adult areas and the children's areas.

Toilets. Look at where they are. They should be fairly close to the group room with a ventilating lobby between for supervision. The ideal thing is to have toilets of varying heights, or one small toilet, but this would again have to be specially installed if the nursery is in a house. Children should have their own pegs for their own flannel and there should be a small bath for emergencies.

Floor plan. The open floor plan is now out of fashion as it is considered too unmanageable for a child to cope with. Each child should have a home base in which he feels at home and safe, where he can identify with the staff and feel secure without being surrounded by too many children. The group rooms should be self-contained for no more than eight to ten children.

Group room. As well as being a home base, it should be large enough for two groups to come together.

Wet play. Are there sinks in the general play area?

Baby room. There should not be more than five cots in the baby room. It is nice to have a milk kitchen off the baby room but not really necessary.

Kitchen. Have a look at the kitchen and make sure that there are adequate guards on the cookers to prevent accidents.

Outdoor space. The ideal space is partly paved and partly grassed and should be equipped with climbing and outdoor play apparatus.

The school itself

Size. There are no regulations governing the size of a nursery school or playgroup. The building or space has to be adequate for the children. The Environmental Health Officer visits every prospective nursery and advises on the maximum number of children allowable. All nurseries must be registered with the local council, so any nursery you visit will have conformed to the requirements. Sessional nurseries tend to be smaller than day-care nurseries. The former are usually for between 15 and 20 children with two to three adults, the latter can be large enough for 50 children. Ideally, a nursery school should not be too large. The number of children relates to the size of the space but few nurseries can take more than 50 children and most cater for between 25 and 30.

Food. Day-care nurseries provide children with breakfast, a hot lunch and tea. Sessional care nurseries provide children with a drink and snack at some time during the three-hour period.

Settling in. 18 months to two years is the most difficult age to settle into a nursery. Parents should try to reserve at least a month to be available to their child settling into the routine of an all-day nursery, staying with him for the first week for a considerable time and then diminishing this over a period of about a month. Follow the advice and guidance of the head of the nursery as to what progress is being made in settling in. The head has been through it before and you haven't.

How are the numbers divided? Some nurseries divide children into what is called a family grouping with children of various age groups making up a group of about eight children. Others divide the children into age groups on the basis that it is unfair to older children to have their work and projects ruined by the interference of younger children, and younger children are intimidated by older children. Listen to the experience and views of the director of the school and make your own decision as to what you think is appropriate.

The staff. The qualifications of the staff depend on the sort of day care provided. A playgroup leader is not expected to have the same sort of qualification as the head of a day nursery. Where the playgroup leader would be expected to have done a play leader's course and have a Pre-School Playgroup Association qualification, the head of a day nursery would be expected to be a qualified nursery nurse with an NNEB, or be a qualified Montessori teacher, or have done a post-qualifying degree. Find out how many of the staff are qualified and ask your Social Services Department what their expectation is as to percentage of staff with a qualification. In general, half the staff should be qualified in some way and the head of the nursery *must* be qualified.

The variety of training and qualifications expected of childcare workers is enormous (see Chapter 3). The staff might be a mix of young girls who have just got their NNEB qualifications and older women whose qualifications for the job are based on long-term experience of working with children. It is nice to see some young men working in a nursery so the children are not exposed exclusively to female care-givers. No specific qualification is essential to work in a nursery. The quality of the staff should be apparent from the atmosphere.

Staff ratios to children. The recommended ratios for care in all-day nurseries is 1 to 3 for infants up to two years old and 1 to 5 from two to five years. This is a high but essential carer to infant ratio which is why nursery care is not cheap. These are the recommended ratios in the 1968 Amendment to the Nurseries and Childminders Regulation Act of 1948 as amended by the Health Services and Public Health Act of 1968. In order to be registered, a nursery school has to comply with the recommended ratios.

Behaviour and discipline. Corporal punishment is no longer an acceptable way of dealing with a problem child. Every nursery school has a different approach. Some nurseries have a naughty chair or a naughty place for children to go to calm down and think quietly about their behaviour towards others. If a child is a real handful, the carers will take it in turns to try to get him to settle in. However, if the child is totally unmanageable, eventually a nursery will ask the parents to withdraw him. One nursery head told me that people used to be frightened to admit to a nursery head that they were having problems at home that might lead to their child having behaviour problems for fear of the child being taken into care. Nowadays, people are much more relaxed about admitting their lives are less than perfect. A child's troubled or bad behaviour is often a reaction to problems at home. A good nursery head knows from the child's behaviour that all is not right at home and will take the time to listen. You must take the time to talk about a situation at home that might be affecting your child's behaviour at the nursery.

Outside activities. Adventures outside the nursery usually relate to the skills of parents and add an extra dimension to the older children's experience. Small children go out much more than they used to to accomplish small tasks, like buying the things they need for a project. Gone is the clinical childcare of a generation ago. Today there are fewer rules and the staff do not feel restricted by a set format. A good staff takes advantage of a sunny day and sets off with young charges on the road to adventure, usually a few yards to the playground round the corner.

Type of child and catchment area. Children tend to be fairly local at a nursery unless it is at a workplace. Mothers who have brought their small babies into work with them usually prefer a local nursery when the child is older, not so easy to carry, and less happy on a long journey into work. Some boroughs sponsor children whose parents would otherwise not be able to afford a nursery place and for whom a place cannot be found in a state nursery. Other boroughs do not have a scheme for sponsorship. The racial mix will depend on the area in which you live. All boroughs have anti-racist policies, boldly stated in their literature. A good mix of children, religion, race, income and shoe size makes a nursery an interesting place and is a good preparation for life.

Older children arriving after school. Most nurseries find that the sudden presence of an older child after school is disruptive, as the older children no longer fit in. The nursery might make an exception of an older sibling on holiday, but generally it is not a good idea to mix much older children with tiny ones.

Collecting and delivering. Ask your husband to deliver the children. Fathers are much better at an unemotional and quick delivery. Mothers very often confuse children, allowing them to turn the small event of being left at the day nursery into a big emotional issue by going back for that extra kiss and cuddle. If your husband takes the children in the morning, and you collect them in the evening, you can indulge in as many extra hugs, kisses and cuddles as you like with no emotional repercussions.

Late collection. This is seldom an option as, if it were, parents would collect their children late every day. The staff are tired and want to get home and the children have come to the end of a long day. In an emergency, a member of staff will be willing to stay on or even take a child home with them, but a nursery expects collection to be punctual. If a parent is consistently late in collecting a child, ultimately the head will probably ask the parent to withdraw the child. It is emotionally very hard on the child to have to wait and wait for a parent who doesn't seem to come after all the other children have gone. The school won't care who collects your child provided they are informed, just so long as it is done punctually.

The ill child. If a child becomes ill during the course of the day, the nursery expects a parent to come and collect the child as soon as possible. It is not reasonable to leave a child who might be contagious in the company of other susceptible small children. The nursery won't think highly of a parent who wants them to hold on to the child so she doesn't have to interrupt her day.

All the above assumes you have been lucky enough to find a suitable place for your child in a day nursery. In fact, there is a desperate shortage of places all over the country.

Workplace nurseries

The Workplace Nurseries Campaign objective is to promote the establishment of nursery facilities near or in the parent's place of work. Workplace nurseries are a good solution when a child is tiny and easily transportable. By the time a child is three, a long car journey to and from work can be an exhausting experience, but even more difficult is a journey on public transport during the rush hour.

After children are two and a half or three years old, many mothers feel that a local nursery is a better solution.

The Workplace Nurseries Campaign

The Campaign was set up in 1984 as a response to the government's decision to tax the subsidy given by the employer for a nursery place by adding the sum to the employee's income. This can put the parent in a higher tax bracket, making the cost too great for the parent to sustain. New mothers are encouraged to join. As a member you receive a regular newsletter and discounts on publications. For information write or telephone the Campaign headquarters at:

77 Holloway Road, London N7 8JZ
Campaign: 01-700 0281
Consultancy: 01-700 0274

A success story

City Child was set up in 1980 by a group of parents interested in lobbying for a City of London-based nursery facility. They raised money by knocking on doors but finding a premises was a considerable problem. The Merrill Lynch Group of Companies wanted to build in Islington and, because Islington Council was sympathetic to City Child's campaign, it implemented a 'planning gain' regarding Merrill Lynch's building and granted planning permission contingent on the inclusion of a nursery. When Merrill Lynch were granted planning permission on these terms, the management council of City Child approached Merrill Lynch and suggested that they run it. Merrill Lynch were only too pleased to accept. They did not have the space to put the nursery on the premises but luckily found alternative premises close by. The agreement was that Islington Council would subsidise the nursery by two-thirds of its cost per parent and advertise the availability of the space to all their staff.

The nursery is located in the heart of the Barbican. Surrounded by old, oppressive office buildings, City Child is in a modern, purpose-built, low building with a cheerful blue door, at the top of a winding ramp. Mothers manoeuvre push-chairs up it and toddlers toddle down it into the outdoor play area with ease. The play area is at the front of the building and, although tiny, contains a climbing frame. I was most impressed with the determination of a two-year-old, waddling like Michelin Man in a snowsuit, making his own way down the ramp, eyes fixed on the play area.

The cost is £415 per calendar month, two-thirds of which is

subsidised by Merrill Lynch for their own employees. Of 26 children in the nursery at present, only five are offspring of Merrill Lynch employees. City Child is non-profit making and, at a little over £100 per week, this seems to be the cost per week per child at state nurseries all over the country. It is open from 8.30 am to 6 pm. There is space for 15 under 2½-year-olds and 15 over 2½-year-olds. At the moment they have six babies (3–18 months) which is the statutory limit, and six 18-month to two-year-olds. The rest are over two. The ratio of staff is 1 to 3 children overall, but in practice there is a higher ratio for the babies than for the older children.

There is a long waiting list for babies, about 40 at present, but no real waiting list for older children. This is possibly because older children are found places close to home.

The staff are paid the going rate for nursery teachers in the state sector; they are all NNEBs.

City Child Day Nursery
1 Bridgewater Square, London EC2Y 8AD; 01-374 0939
Tilly Hamilton – Director

The Midland Bank – thinking ahead

The Midland Bank intends to subsidise three nurseries immediately: one possibly in Beckenham, Greater London, and two definitely in Sheffield and Crawley. Workplace Nurseries was employed by Midland Bank itself to advise, while the moving force in establishing the nurseries were the two banking trade unions, MSF and BIFU. By 1993 the Midland, as a result of their own initiative and in conjunction with other companies and local authorities, propose to open 300 more nurseries.

Susan Hay was part of Workplace Nurseries and has since, with two partners, set up her own consultancy called

Susan Hay Associates
Omnibus Workspace, 41 North Road, London N7 2DP; 01-700 1254

They could be used as consultants by a group of mothers trying to set up a nursery facility in their workplace. The consultancy would advice on how to present their case to their employers. Susan Hay made a point of stressing that her consultancy is not just about workplace nurseries but about the whole problem of children in the environment.

Chapter 5

Childminding

The major problem with childminding is that it involves full-time exhausting work with few career prospects and not much status. For a mother to refer to her childcarer as a 'nanny' is loaded with status. Taking the child to the minder is not.

The National Childminding Association (NCMA) was set up in 1977 by a group of childminders, parents and childcare workers in the belief that any move to improve the quality of day care must be beneficial. Training materials are available and childminders are encouraged to join together for support, training and exchange of resourses.

NCMA issues a wide range of publications for both the minder and parents. Make sure that your minder is aware of and up to date with the advances in her profession. Send for the booklets yourself so you know what to expect.

National Childminding Association
8 Masons Hill, Bromley, Kent BR2 9EY; 01-464 6164

If you phone, the Bromley office will inform you who your regional representative is. She will help you in any way she can.

What is a childminder?

A childminder is someone who takes care of a child to whom she is not related for more than two hours a day and is paid to do so. She must be registered with the Social Services Department of the local authority, under the Nursery and Childminders Act 1948 as amended by the Health Service and Public Health Act 1968. She must be over 18 and is usually under 55, with some exceptions.

The local Social Services Department checks the minder and her house for suitability. The Department will have sent a childminding adviser to the minder to counsel and inform. The adviser remains a source of information to the minder and the Social Services Department itself may provide training courses and toy and equipment loan schemes. By registering, the minder is put in contact with other minders. Some authorities will let a minder take in more children if she is experienced or has a helper.

By law she is not allowed to have more than three children in her care under five, including under-fives of her own or a fostered child, and not more than one of the children should be under 18 months. If she has a registered helper she should not have more than six children under the age of five.

Two or more women can become registered in one premises to look after a group of children not exceeding seven. Registration conditions are the same but conditions set by the Environmental and Fire Officers must be met as this is treated as a small group.

The most general complaint about childminding is that the quality of the child's existence is low because the child is not stimulated during the day. This is because there are no set standards and qualifications to being a minder; she is not a trained play leader and has to get on with running her own house as well as minding the child. It is up to you to decide whether the minder who you choose is, in your estimation and by your yardstick, 'a fit person'.

NCMA produces a leaflet, 'Guidelines on Pay and Conditions', which all members receive free of charge but the rate you pay depends on the region in which you live and on all the extras, from providing nappies to taking the children on outings, that the childminder provides for your baby. The question of money should be settled at the outset and a contract should be agreed to and signed. NCMA provides contract forms as do Social Service Departments. This saves hurt and embarrassment at a later stage when you have developed a good relationship with the minder and your baby is happy with her.

How to find a childminder

Contact your local Social Services Department who will give you a list of childminders with vacancies in your area. Do this before the baby is born when you have the time and can take a relaxed attitude. Visit as many minders as you like, but certainly more than one, so that you have a good idea of what it is you want and what is available.

The National Childminding Association will send you all kinds of information aimed at both the minder and the parents. Study the leaflets on finding a childminder.

The Social Services Department will tell you what the local going rate is, but you must make your own arrangement with the minder based on time and services.

The Social Services Department will only recommend a child-minder who is registered as it is not legal to be a childminder and not be registered. She will have been visited by someone in the Department and satisfy the criteria for childminders.

What to ask and notice at the minder's

- Is she warm and welcoming? Does she make you feel at ease and comfortable?
- Are you able to discuss your feelings about leaving your child? Does she talk about herself and what she has to offer?
- Does she respond warmly to your child?
- Ask the minder if she has taken any of the courses offered for minders and what her general experience is in caring for children.
- Look around the house and take note of the atmosphere, the toys, the safety precautions like stair gates and fire guards.
- Are there books and stimulating materials about? (Child-minders may borrow up to 30 books at a time for up to three months through the library service.)
- Is there outside play space?
- Ask the minder what sort of outdoor activities your child will experience. Will he go shopping, to the library, to the park, to other local childminder groups, to local parent and toddler groups, drop-in centres or one o'clock clubs? Is there a local sports centre that has a baby bounce or a toddler swimming session? Find out if she takes the children with her if she collects older children from school. If she takes the children in the car, does she have seat belts for the children in the back?
- Ask her if she is a member of NCMA and carries their insurance. Has she, by the way, taken any of their courses?
- Find out what sort of first aid and medical knowledge she has.
- Observe her with the other children. Is she natural and relaxed? Does she talk and play?
- Do you get a sense of order and structure about her day?
- Is the house warm and light?
- What is the toilet like?
- Talk to her about settling your baby in. Find out what she expects of you and how she expects you to make the adjust-

ment. How long will she expect you to stay at first? Ask how long it usually takes a baby to get used to being left.

- Discipline is an important matter to resolve. Allow her to discipline the child in her home even when you are there so the child knows who is in charge, and when, and doesn't play you off against each other.
- Ask her what sort of food she gives the children and discuss with her your own views on healthy fare. You won't be happy if your child is plied with stodge all day, but the childminder won't be happy if asked to ply the child with nothing but expensive fruit, fish and meat. You can only come to an understanding if you make your feelings known.
- What is her attitude to toilet training?
- Does the minder want to visit you to find out what your home is like?
- How flexible is the childminder? She can care for the sibling of a child in her care in an emergency, but she must notify the Department and they must confirm the temporary arrangement. If the extra child overlaps by more than two hours, her insurance must be adjusted.
- How flexible is she when you have to stay late at the office? Make sure you come to a clear understanding. How does your minder feel about overtime? Is she fairly relaxed or very strict? If something holds you up, will you arrive to find your child has been standing in the hall in a snow-suit for the last one and a half hours?
- Does she have more children after school? There is no statutory ruling on over-fives staying with a minder after school. There should not be more than three including the minder's own children. Make sure a mob doesn't descend at 3.30 on school holidays and at half term. The effect on the under-fives of over-fives is not necessarily bad but can affect the general quality of care.

Remember, it is important that you visit more than one childminder in order to know exactly what it is that pleases and appeals to you.

Once you have found a minder

- Make sure everything is 'up front' and understood.
- Do you both agree on the arrangements for settling in your child?

- Have you agreed on payment and method of payment? This is important as it is likely to be your minder's only source of income. What about payment during your holiday? She must have a guarantee of payment regardless of what changes you might make in your plans. Have you agreed regular increases, sick pay, overtime pay, holiday pay?
- What arrangements have you made if the minder is ill, if your child is ill or if one of the other children in her care is ill?
- Make sure you have agreed on general delivery and collection times and always inform her if there is going to be any change.
- Agree on the basics at the outset and even write them down if they are not part of the contract. Make sure there is a clear understanding as regards: fees, hours of work, diet, toys, potty training, naps during the day, and overtime that might be required. It is essential to develop an easy, honest and straight-forward relationship with the minder.
- *Insurance*. Make sure your childminder is insured. A reduced premium has been specially negotiated with Phoenix Assurance Company for registered minders who are members of NCMA.
- Not all minding arrangements work out. She may not be right for you or you and your child may not be right for her. Don't be discouraged if an arrangement doesn't work out.

Parents on the whole complain very little about minders and rarely report a minder as being inadequate. Feedback from mothers and other minders is hard to get and, without this feedback, monitoring what is going on is difficult. The statutory provision is for only two visits a year (without forewarning) to check on the 'fitness' of a person to be a minder. Help your local Social Services Department by keeping them informed as to the quality of the minder you use and anything you disapprove of.

The childminder also needs to know about you

- Be open with the minder so that she has a good knowledge of your baby's parents. After all, she is going to develop a close relationship with him and she will not only be interested in background details of his life but need to know them to understand the pressures and stresses of your life that might affect the child.
- Tell her your and your husband's occupations and make sure

she has your work address and telephone and a few other contact numbers in case of emergency.

- Make sure she has your baby's medical history and the name of your family doctor.
- If your child has any allergies or special dietary needs, make sure she knows about them.
- Let your minder know the names and phone numbers of anyone who might collect your child beside your husband and yourself. Make sure she understands she must never allow your child to be collected by anyone other than you or your husband without specific instructions that this is all right.

The contract

It is vital, no matter how trusting and confident you are with your minder, that the agreement made is legally recorded in a contract. The National Childminding Association has drawn up a one-page form as a 'Record of Information about a Minded Child'. The Parent and Childminder Agreement on pages 65–67 is a thorough and comprehensive document and a model of the sort of contract you should have with your minder.

Courses for childminders

Haringey in north London is a good example of a cosmolitan area. It is large, polyglot and contains areas of every income level and social class. It has a particularly caring Social Services Department. In Haringey there are more unregistered childminders than registered. The borough encourages minders to register by, among other things, advertising days of 'amnesty' in local newspapers for illegal minders to come and register. Haringey requires preregistration training for minders. Haringey also offers college training for minders. By participating in such courses, the minder is able to network with other minders, develop a sense of professionalism and status and view her role as a minder as a career.

Make sure you are aware of what sort of preparation is expected of childminders in your area by calling the Social Services Department for your borough or district and asking for the Day-Care Co-ordinator for the under-fives.

NCMA offers courses and there are even Open University courses for minders.

■ HARINGEY COUNCIL ■

Parent & Childminder Agreement

For Childminders registered with the London Borough of Haringey

(One copy should be kept by the Parent and one by the Childminder
This Agreement only remains valid whilst the childminder complies with her conditions of Registration
and when signed by them is binding on both parties)

1. CHILD'S FULL NAME .... DATE OF BIRTH ....
   HOME ADDRESS ....
   ....
   .... TELEPHONE NO ....
   WORK ADDRESS .... TELEPHONE NO ....

2. ATTENDANCE:

Days		Arrival Time	Leaving Time	Hours
Monday	....	....	....	....
Tuesday	....	....	....	....
Wednesday	....	....	....	....
Thursday	....	....	....	....
Friday	....	....	....	....

3. FEES: ....per week on Monday in advance.

   a) A Registration Fee of one week's money is payable when agreement is reached to care for the child — this fee is regarded as the payment of the first week's fee.

   b) See Appendix 1 regarding part-time fees.
   Part-time fee agreed (where applicable)..............................

   c) The fee remains the same if the child is absent (e.g. through illness).

   d) The fee will be reviewed, at least, annually and one month's notice will be given of any increase.

4. RETAINING FEE: Should there be a delay between agreement to care for the child and the starting date a retaining fee of.................per week is payable. (Half fee is suggested)

5. OVERTIME: Payable at.................per half hour. (A suggested 1½ times your normal rate)

6. HOLIDAYS:

   a) Holiday Arrangement Forms should be completed when holidays are agreed. (See attached forms. One copy to be retained by Parent and one by Minder.)

   b) The Minder is entitled to three weeks holiday per year on full pay, plus all Public Holidays, and the days between Boxing Day and New Year's Day.

   c) The Minder will attempt to give four three months notice of her annual holidays. It is better for the child if parents can take their holidays at the same time as the Minder. If this is not possible the Minder will try to make alternative arrangements for you with a Registered Childminder with the agreement and help of Social Services. Minders are entitled to claim up to one week sick pay in any one year.

   d) If you child starts with, or leaves, a Minder part of the way through the year, holidays should be paid proportionally — i.e. one week's holiday pay for four month's minding ''possible the Minder may be able to help you make...................................

   e) If Parents take more than three weeks holiday. the Minder must be paid at the full rate for the first three weeks and a mutual agreement may be reached at the time regarding payment for the remainder of the holiday (see Appendix 2)

   Agreement reached (where applicable)

7. **PARENTS TO BRING:** Nappies — YES/NO   Food — YES/NO
It is advisable that bottles are prepared and brought by Parent.
Other items e.g. clothing..

8. **MEALS PROVIDED:** BREAKFAST — LUNCH — TEA

9. **SICKNESS:** If your child has been sick during the night you <u>must</u> inform the Minder so she can decide whether to admit your child or not. She has other children to care for that may be in danger of being infected. If the child has had an infectious illness the parent should give the Minder a Doctor's letter when the child is returned to her care indicating that the infection is now clear.

If your child has any medicine prescribed by a Doctor, the Minder must be informed in case of side effects and permission given to administer medicine — signature.................................

The childminder is not expected to give minded child anything other than the prescribed medicine.

The Minder must inform the parents if there has been any sickness in her household and parents are not expected to pay for consequent days of absence by the child.

10. **URGENT MEDICAL TREATMENT:** I give permission for my child...to receive urgent

medical treatment if Ms...is unable to contact me.

Signed...

Parent(s)
....

11. **NOTICE:** Two weeks' notice to be given by Parent or Minder, or money in lieu. Notice will not be required in the first two weeks as these weeks are considered a trial period for both Minder and Parent/Child and where the minding arrangement is ended in these circumstances any money already paid for days when the child is not minded should be refunded. Your Minder is entitled to up to one week — i.e. 5 days paid sick leave in any one year.

12. **MINDER'S NOTICE** Under no circumstances must less than two weeks notice be given, if any emergency arises it should be discussed with the day care officer.

I agree to care for your child...

in accordance with the conditions set out above from...(date)

Signed...   (Minder)

Name (in block letters)...

Address...

....

....

Date ....

I have read the conditions set out above, understand them and agree to abide by this Agreement.

Signed...

Parents

....

Name (in block letters)...

Address...

....

....

Date ....

The form of this Agreement was approved by the Haringey Childminding Association and Haringey Social Services Department

3/83

APPENDIX — Recommendation

1. The question of fees for part-time children may be decided upon by determining whether the part time hours are effectively preventing you from earning full time money. If this is the case it is advisable to charge full time money. If, however, you care for, say, two children part time (perhaps one in the morning and one in the afternoon) then of course half fee for each child would be appropriate. Fees are, of course, always a matter for the Parent and Minder to reach agreement on.

2. Many Childminders care for Schoolteachers' children and are unsure what to charge for holidays. As the Schoolteacher receives full pay for holidays the Minder is entitled to expect the same, although you may wish to come to an arrangement for a lower fee for perhaps half of the long summer holiday — the first three weeks to count as your annual holiday pay.

3. Each Childminder should use their Agreement Form to suit each individual case — any points on the Agreement may be altered where necessary for each situation.

   Alterations should be signed by both Parent and Minder and dated.

   When agreement is reached to change the fee charged it is advisable to complete a fresh Agreement form.

4. It is advisable for Childminders to issue receipts to parents each time payment is received for the care of the child, one copy for the parent and one copy for the Minder — specifying amount paid and the dates covered by the payment.

Special Note

The London Borough of Haringey has its own scheme for paying Childminders who agree to mind children referred to them by the Council. This is called the "Sponsorship Scheme" and the details are shown on the final page of this document.

- -

HOLIDAY ARRANGEMENT FORM

CHILD'S NAME...

Dates of holiday

From (first day of absence from Minder)..

To (date of return to Minder)..

Signed ....(Parent)

Signed..(Minder)

Date ....

- -

Reprinted with permission of Haringey Social Services Department

Talking with childminders

Earnings

Minders in north London charge between £40 and £45 per week for a child. The cost varies greatly throughout the country. In Aberdeen, for example, minders are paid on average £1.25 per hour which works out at about £63 per week. Costs have risen sharply in the last 12 years. None of the minders calculated exactly what their expenses including food cost them. When you work out that they are giving the children three meals a day, this is a very small amount of money to be paid – less than £1 an hour for each child, excluding expenses. Parents were expected to bring disposable nappies and a flannel and the minders don't do any of the children's laundry.

Combination agony aunt, psychologist, counsellor and social worker

My questions about the mothers' psychological state were almost always met with the comment that by the end of the week the mothers were exhausted. When children suddenly became difficult, it was usually the parents who had the problems and they often wanted to unburden themselves to the minder. You could see immediately if there were problems by the behaviour of the child. It made no difference whether the parents were professional people or not. Some people are good at handling the stress of organising their lives and some are not. Some mothers were traumatised by having to leave their babies. The minders were well aware of the stress for mothers of having the baby, running the home and perhaps having a non-supportive partner. Many minders reported having to calm tearful mothers.

Joint minding

Everyone felt this was not a good idea as children might get short shrift.

Minding v nursery school

All the minders were convinced that minding was better for the child because of the regularity of care and the home environment. Two or three children keep one another entertained.

Times of minding

The minders who charge more mind for longer hours, from 8 am to 6 pm, as opposed to 8 am to 5 pm. The hours depend on the profession of the parents. Teachers in particular have a shorter working day. The minders all said they would allow for some leeway with collection time, provided it is not consistently late. The children have a long day and often sleep a lot when they are small.

Jealousy

This was not considered a problem, as the minders were not trying to be surrogate parents and were called either auntie or their first names by the children. Kissing and cuddling only happens if the child needs it, not because they want or need to cuddle the children. A good understanding of the family is essential, and some of the minders took time to visit parents at their home when first approached, and asked the parents to visit them during the day to see the set-up with the children. Their own children are not jealous of the minded children because they know that, when the children leave, their mother is all theirs.

Settling in

The mother visits with her child for coffee for an hour or so. Most minders prefer to have a child for a trial period before signing the contract. The mother should bring the child at least three times and then leave the child for short periods by himself. It usually takes about six weeks for a child to settle in and relax.

Food

All the minders were aware of the necessity of a good diet and giving their charges a hot lunch. There is no difficulty coping with special diets, be they kosher or vegetarian. Whether a child is fed properly often has little to do with the family income. Parents supply any unusual food. Most children arrive having only had a glass of juice in the morning. The parents are thus relieved of all the work of feeding the children.

Holidays

Minders give parents three months' notice of their three-week annual holiday and are paid the full amount during those three weeks. They also have all the public holidays and are paid for the full week. If the parents are teachers and have long summer holidays as well as Christmas and Easter, an agreement is come to whereby half the summer holiday is the minder's annual holiday, through which she is paid in full. During the other half, she would be paid half her rate by the parents in order to keep the place.

Chapter 6

Agencies and Nannies

Agencies

A nanny or au pair agency is an employment agency like any other and must be licensed by the Employment Agency Licensing Office which is part of the Department of Employment.

Employment Agency Licensing Office
2–16 Church Road, Stanmore, Middlesex HA7 4AW; 01-954 7677

The requirements needed to get a licence are not such that the agency is guaranteed to be efficient. However, they are enough to show good intent. An agency is required to display a notice on the premises for three weeks and to put an advertisement in a weekly newspaper indicating the intention to open an agency. At the end of three weeks, the Licensing Office will ask for three personal references, a CV of what the person applying has been doing for the last ten years, and will make enquiries regarding the applicant to employers of the last five years. If the Office is satisfied with the applicant, it will grant a licence, renewable annually for the fee of £114. After six months an inspector will call to make sure that correct records are being kept and subsequently will inspect annually.

All employment agencies are subject to the Employment Agency Act 1973, chapter 35, and the Regulations on Running an Agency (Statutory Instrument 1976 – No 715). Statutory Instrument 1981 No 1481 specifically relates to charging fees to au pairs. These documents are available from HMSO; 01-622 3316.

Use a reliable agency – one that has a reputation, and one that fills you with confidence when you deal with it. Before you start to deal with an agency, obtain its terms of business so that you know beforehand the agency's responsibilities to you and the girl, as well as their fees.

Domestic employment agencies specialise in a particular area. Those providing childcarers will be able to recommend maternity nurses, nannies, mother's helps and, in some cases, au pairs and

71

governesses. They may also place domestic helps and other household staff such as chauffeurs and butlers.

Rather than state specifically at the outset that you want a nanny or an au pair, take the time to describe to the agency what exactly your needs are. The agency will then advise you on what sort of help you actually need. You may think you want a nanny but find what you really have in mind is a mother's help or an au pair. The agency might recommend a type of help that you haven't even considered; for example, a maternity nurse to tide you over the first six weeks of the baby's life.

On the other hand, you may want the baby all to yourself for the first six weeks, and really need a devoted slave to take care of everything else in the house. None of the agencies I spoke to had anyone on their books described as a 'slave', but if you explain the situation, the agency should be able to help you out.

Maternity nurses

A maternity nurse is a woman who has decided to specialise in short-term contracts taking care of new-born babies and does not wish to stay with the family for longer than three months at most. The usual period is from four to six weeks. Women who specialise in maternity nursing are women who prefer working with tiny babies as opposed to toddlers or older children.

Agencies vary as to the qualifications they demand from maternity nurses. All maternity nurses from Baby Company are nursery nurses with NNEB qualifications. They have worked on a maternity ward and have experience with premature babies and caesarians. They may also be general nurses but they have definitely had specific nursing training. Furthermore, the Baby Company does not employ anyone under the age of 24.

On the other hand, Juliet Chapple from Knightsbridge Nannies said that they do not demand that the nurse has an NNEB certificate but she must have three or four years' experience. Juliet had a more relaxed attitude towards qualifications but charged less. She felt that people now tend to prefer a young or younger girl because they want flexibility and the maternity nurses of the old school tend to be dogmatic in their approach. However, I suspect that most of the traditional nurses have by now gone to the great nursery in the sky, and how dictatorial a contemporary maternity nurse is depends entirely on her personality. A total dragon would not find many jobs.

When engaging a maternity nurse through an agency, you sign a contract with the agency.

The maternity nurse is on duty 24 hours a day, six days a week. She is totally in charge of the baby, doing all the night feedings, her role being to establish a good routine for the baby.

Peace of mind is what you are paying for and it is expensive. The maternity nurse is paid well, anything from £160 to £300 per week depending on a number of factors:

- her experience
- number of children (twins for example)
- time of year (over Christmas period)

British Nursing Association Carers provide fully trained nurses as maternity nurses who are paid on a daily basis of £46.19 per day which works out at £277.14 for a six-day week (1989).

Harry at Baby Company recommended booking them well in advance, say, six months before the due date of the baby. Juliet at Knightsbridge Nannies said it was not necessary to book more than a few months in advance because often a baby is either early or late and the nurse finds she has been booked for the wrong time and has to cancel one mother or other.

The agencies I spoke to reported that about 50% of their clients are working mothers but that was only an estimate as none had ever kept statistics. Before the baby is born, many mothers with careers think that they will return to work immediately. There is a noticeable trend for them either to change their minds at the outset or to return to work and realise that they don't want to leave their babies. Juliet at Knightsbridge Nannies has had many instances of maternity nurses and nannies being cancelled for that reason.

Objections. Mothers can feel that the maternity nurse is too dictatorial and takes over her role as mother entirely. Since she is on duty 24 hours a day, it is not difficult for the mother to distance herself from her new-born baby. Then the question of with whom the baby has bonded arises. Also, unless you have someone else doing all the housework and cooking, you will find that the maternity nurse is spending her day getting all the joy and pleasure out of the new baby that should be yours, while you keep the rest of the household in order. You may decide that what you want is not a maternity nurse, but someone to do everything else *but* look after the new-born baby.

You will find agencies in the Yellow Pages, in *Nursery World* and

The Lady. The following agencies have given me information about maternity nurses.

Baby Company
168 Sloane Street, London SW1X 9QF
01-581 8171

British Nursing Association Carers
Head Office, 443 Oxford Street, London W1A 2NR
01-629 9030

Kensington & Chelsea Nurses & Nannies
2nd Floor, 168 Sloane Street, London SW1X 9QF
01-589 2093 and 01-259 6721

Knightsbridge Nannies
5 Beauchamp Place, London SW3 1NG
01-584 9323

The Nicest Nannies
51 Connaught Gardens, London N10 3LG
01-444 1928

The nanny

This is not the Victorian age where, if the nanny loses her job, she is out on the street. Nowadays you are doing well to keep someone for a year and very well if you keep her for two. You won't keep her for a year if she isn't happy. It has become such a sellers' market that nannies ring up the agent and specify what they want down to the finest detail. A potential employee who has the upper hand in choosing a job feels no compunction about stating her needs. Agencies have got used to hearing the likes of 'I want no more than two children, and no babies, definitely the use of the car, and the couple must be young and casual. I won't accept a job without my own bath but I would really like my own flat.'

Where to find a nanny

Advertisements
A glance at the Situations Vacant columns in *The Lady* and the Jobs with Families columns in *Nursery World* is enough to chill the most optimistic heart. However, good nannies can be found through

perseverance and diligence and knowing exactly what you want.

The Lady
Nursery World
Local newspapers
Local magazines
National newspapers

Agencies

What you should expect to pay the agency. Agencies will charge you £25 to register and then charge a fee for placing a nanny with you. This fee will vary according to the amount of time the nanny is intended to stay with you. However, it will not be less than £300 and should not be more than about £750.

What you should expect to pay the nanny. A probabtionary nanny who has not completed her nine months' residential work and doesn't yet have her full diploma and badge would expect to be paid no less than £75 gross per week. After she is fully qualified, she would expect no less than £110 per week, but the current average for a full-time nanny is about £140 gross per week depending on the part of the country. The top gross salary can be as much as £210 per week, but outside London it would be unusual for a nanny to earn more than £160. The better the salary, the easier it is to attract applicants for the job. Offer a reasonable salary with good conditions and two days off per week.

With horror you may find yourself paying almost all your salary on childcare. Think of this situation, which will not last for ever, as an investment in the future. You are deferring the gratification of enjoying all the money you will earn from developing a career until later. The investment in good childcare will allow you to enjoy the quality of your career and your home life a great deal more when you know you have provided the best when it was important.

Two years of a caring and loving nanny are worth their weight in gold compared to constantly changing both your ideas of what you want and the person who fulfils that idea. In the happiness area, the most important people to consider are not the nanny or yourself but your children. Constant change and strife around their carer and your arrangements will render them confused and insecure. Remember, they are the only children you will ever have and this is the only childhood they will ever have. Make it a good one and keep that in mind all the time you are organising care for them.

Liability. Remember that the agency is not liable for any action of the nanny. The agency service is solely the introduction. However, the residential colleges keep tabs on their graduates, holding information on both the nanny and the family and will help with difficulties.

From the agencies' point of view. Most clients have a prepared speech about themselves which they give over the phone to the agency which reveals to the agent much more about the client than the client ever learns about the agency.

There is the 'I want a nanny who' followed by a precise regimen and high expectations but concluding with 'and she must be doing the job for the love of the children'. This indicates to the agent that the client will work the girl to death and pay her as little as possible. Why a mother thinks someone else should take care of her children for love, when she herself isn't prepared to do so, is a mystery agencies have been trying to solve for years. It is a sad fact that many people have the idea that carers, even if the caring is for their own children, are somehow low-status workers and do not need to be paid much.

The slightly uncertain client will often be the best employer. After giving personal details this client will ask what sort of help the agent thinks she needs. In this case the agent will advise whether a nanny or a mother's help is most suitable. Often a mother's help will be sent to people who have originally asked for a nanny because they really need a maid-of-all-work who will muck in with everything.

Types of family and types of nanny. The upstairs-downstairs approach is not a natural or usual sort of relationship to develop in this day and age. A nanny wants to feel that she is a professional and deserves the respect of any employer. Nevertheless, she may well have a contemporary attitude to wearing a uniform and terms of address. Norland suggest that their nannies are called 'Nurse and then the first or second name'. This is entirely up to you and the girl. She may want to wear a uniform and be called 'Nurse Jones', or she may want to wear a track suit and be called 'Sally'. If she wears a uniform, she expects the family to help her with the expense (about £20 per annum).

The four most frequently described types of family are: old money, professional couple efficient, professional couple shambolic, and new money. The professional couple efficient have been reported as the easiest to get along with.

The agent will ask if the client has had a nanny before and will always listen to feedback from a nanny regarding the family and the house.

The interview. Unlike an au pair coming from abroad, a nanny or mother's help is available for an interview.

What to ask about. Set up a cosy situation and find out everything there is to know about the girl: education, family background, what her parents do, how many siblings she has and where she fits in, training, feelings about the job, interest in children, future ambitions, personal habits (does she smoke or not – ask her even if you have specified a non-smoker to the agency), does she drive and is her licence clean, does she have a boyfriend and if so what does he do and where does he live, hobbies, attitude to discipline and general approach to child development.

Volunteer information about yourself and your family: your husband's and your professions, your family, its size and where the grandparents and close relatives live, how often you visit them, the format of your day, holidays and trips abroad, how often you are away, what the family hobbies are, pets, your own attitudes to discipline and how to bring up children, your religion or lack of it, how much responsibility you expect her to take on and what you are used to the nanny being in charge of.

Explain her duties carefully

Set up hypothetical situations and ask her what she would do. Explain her duties very carefully. At the end of the interview discuss how much time off the nanny would have and when, what her starting salary would be and how often this will be reviewed and increased.

A nanny is not an au pair or a mother's help. She does not expect to muck in where necessary. As a nanny, she has a very clear-cut brief as to her duties and they centre exclusively on the children.

'That is not within my brief': danger lurks at the kitchen sink

At home the nanny will keep the nursery or playroom tidy and clean up after her charges, but she will not clean up after anyone else. This is the thin edge of the wedge as far as nanny's tidying up responsibilities are concerned. The nanny who puts your dirty cup and plate aside in the kitchen sink to clean her own is not crazy. She is making a most important point about the rising spiral of responsibilities and what she does not intend to take on. A cup washed once is a cup for ever waiting to be washed and a nanny who is aware of the danger will make sure you understand the parameters of her duties. She will clean, wash, iron and shop but only if it relates to her charges.

- *She will* tidy the play area, scrub the children's bath, stock the kitchen with nursery food and prepare the nursery meals, wash, iron and maintain the children's clothes, call the repairman to fix the washer and drier and make sure the pram and the push-chair are not on the verge of complete collapse.
- *She will not* tidy the rest of the house, do your weekly shop at the supermarket, cook for your dinner party, organise and supervise the overhaul of your central heating system and oversee the annual servicing of the car.

A mother who is used to handing over domestic organisation to her husband may try to hand over these responsibilities to the nanny. The nanny will resist or expect to be paid commensurately for her additional responsibilities.

References: yours and hers

Get references both from her previous employers and from her college if she has an NNEB. Always follow a reference up by a telephone call. Don't assume, because you have the name of someone, that she will automatically say nice things about the girl. Two or three thorough chats with previous employers or tutors can give you a much better picture of the girl than what you have learned at the interview.

Give the girl the names and telephone numbers of previous nannies. This is both reassuring to the girl and supplies her with the same sort of inside information on you that you would like on her.

In a wealthy family, the nanny might find herself being interviewed by another member of the household before she ever sees the mother. In the job, she would be part of a team running the household. Some girls might find this tremendously glamorous whereas others want a more relaxed kind of job and a more intimate relationship with the family.

Experience counts for a lot. Families are often inclined to hire girls whom they like regardless of whether they have formal qualifications. To many employers, experience is more important than training.

When to decide

An employer should try to have two interviews; first, alone with the girl and then, if she likes her and thinks she might be suitable for the whole family, a second to see how she responds to the children and the children respond to her. Prepare your children for the interview by telling them that you are considering the girl they are going to meet as their next nanny. Explain carefully about interviewing so that they understand what is going on and tell them, no matter how much they like the girl, that they shouldn't say in front of her whether they would like her to come and live with you or not. If they are not old enough to understand, they shouldn't say anything; then they are unlikely to say something that puts you on the spot.

Choosing the nanny as a family event

You will know what your feelings are, but you won't know what the nanny's impression of your household and family is until you offer her the job. Make sure that you and your husband agree before offering a job. One career woman I interviewed told me that her husband was always present and had a say in the hiring of the nanny, but that in the end she made the final decision. She then went on to say how they had had a nanny for five years whom her husband disliked intensely. There isn't much point in having your husband and children present if their feelings are discounted in the final decision.

Don't put the girl on the spot by offering her the job immediately unless you have a clear indication that there is no hesitation and she is not considering other jobs as well. The nanny might be shy about accepting or refusing an immediate job offer.

The live-in versus the live-out nanny

Most experienced nannies prefer to live out, working specific hours usually from 8 or 8.30 am to 6.30 pm with their charges fed, bathed and in their pyjamas before they go. The live-in nanny's hours tend to be longer, usually from when she gets up at 7 am, to 7 pm when her employers come home. Living out gives a nanny real privacy, the chance to have her own private life, and the chance to claim for extra time which is easily calculable. There is a terrible temptation to take advantage of a live-in nanny and she knows it. Extra time is difficult to calculate and resentment can grow unless you have a very straightforward agreement and keep accurate records. Have a clear understanding but better still, *have a contract*.

The contract

Study the Norland contract below. It includes all the obvious. It is always an excellent idea if you are making up your own contract to have a brainstorming session with your husband and/or a friend who has had nannies before to list everything that is not obvious, eliminate the silly things, and add the rest to your contract.

Conditions of Employment for Probationary Nursery Nurse placed through the Norland Registry

Name and Address of Employer:

Name of Employee:

Date of Commencement of Employment:

Job Title: Probationary Nursery Nurse

Remuneration   Your salary is £   gross per week, payable weekly/monthly in arrears. Tax and National Insurance contributions are to be deducted by me/us from this sum. You will be provided with a written statement of your monthly/weekly pay, stating gross pay, statutory deductions and net pay. There will be a salary review after   months employment, and you will be advised in writing of any increase in pay. In the event of unauthorised absence, the right is reserved to withhold salary on a basis pro rata to days lost.

Likely duration of post   As a Probationary Norland Nurse, it is our intention that you remain in my/our employ for a period of NINE months, at the end of which time I/we will complete and return a report form on your work, to The Principal, Norland Nursery Training College. If it is agreed between us that you remain in this post as a Qualified Norland Nurse, your terms of employment will be re-negotiated.

Hours of work   Employment in a private household is such that it is very difficult to define hours of work and free time. However, you will be allowed   free days per week, free from   to   . These hours of work can only be changed by mutual agreement. In addition you will be allowed   weeks paid holiday during the Nine month Probationary Period. Paid compensation is not normally given for holidays not actually taken. Holidays can only be carried into the next year with my/our express permission. You will be free on all Bank Holidays, or will receive a day off or payment in lieu, by agreement.

Sickness   We/I will pay sick benefit   at the rates stipulated by the Government. Your qualifying days for SSP will be Monday to Friday. In addition, I/we will make up the sickness benefit payable under the SSP Scheme to the normal level of your salary, for the first four weeks of sickness if you have been employed for more than thirteen weeks, but less than one year.

Absence through sickness   If you are unable to work through sickness or injury, you must report this to me/us by 10 a.m. on the first day of absence. No Medical Certificate is required for periods of illness of less than Seven Days. A Doctor's Certificate is required when absence due to illness extends to eight days or longer. Except when a Doctor's Certificate is given for longer periods, a Certificate should be produced at weekly intervals.

Termination   In the first four weeks of employment, one week's notice is required on either side. After four weeks continuous service, either the employee or employer may terminate this contract by giving four weeks notice.

Confidentiality   It is a condition of employment that, now and at all times in the future, you keep secret the affairs and concerns of the household and its transactions and business.

Pensions   I/we do/do not run a Pension Scheme. Details are attached if applicable.

P.T.O.

Discipline	Reasons which might give rise for the need for disciplinary measures include the following:
	a) Causing a disruptive influence in the household
	b) Job incompetence
	c) Unsatisfactory standard of dress or appearance
	d) Conduct during or outside working hours, prejudicial to the interests or reputation of the employer
	e) Unreliability in time-keeping or attendance
	f) Failure to comply with instructions and procedure

If it is necessary to take disciplinary action, the procedure will be: Firstly — An oral warning. Secondly — a written warning (Copy to The Principal, Norland Nursery Training College). Thirdly — Dismissal (Notification to be sent immediately to The Principal, Norland N.T.C.). Reasons which might give rise to summary dismissal include: (a) Theft and (b) Drunkenness.

Grievances   If you have any grievances against me/us, you have the right to go direct to The Principal, Norland N.T.C.

Expenses   Approved travel and out of pocket expenses incurred in the course of your employment with this family, will be refunded.

Allowances   An allowance of £   will be paid to you towards the upkeep and repair of the uniform, during the nine month period.

Use of Employer's/ Employee's Car   Details attached (See paragraph 5 in attached leaflet).

The above terms of employment are acceptable to both employer and employee.

....
Signed by Employer   *Signed by Employee*

Date..

Reprinted with the kind permission of Mrs Louise E. Davis,
College Principal of Norlands

The contract should be friendly but with a general understanding of: length of contract, duties, hours, a complete job description, salary and salary reviews, tax etc, holdiays, time off, sick pay, do's and don'ts in the house and everything you can think of without making it too formal and daunting. Be brave and put in details about no boyfriends overnight, no drinking while on duty, no taking the car without asking, and everything else you think is relevant. In any job, a complete job description is essential and nannying is no exception.

Accommodation

A nanny expects to have her own room with a colour television and either her own bath or one she shares only with the children.

The best and most popular accommodation is self-contained with its own kitchenette. This ensures the girl's privacy in the evening. Without the facility for making coffee, the girl is often nabbed while she is in the kitchen and asked to do something. If the girl feels a terrible pressure to go out every evening to ensure that it is a genuine evening off, she is not ultimately going to be happy with the relationship.

The car

Most nannies expect the use of the car if it is available. You wouldn't let her drive your children around if she weren't a competent driver. Trust her. Having the use of a second car gives her status, particularly if she is allowed to drive it home to visit her family.

Status

Many nannies describe what they feel keenly as the lack of career prospects and the stigma of being a nanny as though the job amounted to absolutely nothing. A fair number of nannies told me that they eventually decide to lie and tell people they did all manner of things except be a nanny because it is so embarrassing. However, the term nanny is the most used and the most popular. The Americans, always ready with a euphemism, and ever aware of status, have been devoting considerable effort to finding the right job description for nannies for whom there is currently great demand in the career-crazed US. In-home childcare specialist is the current favourite, but I fear it is too big a mouthful to last. The matter of status is important. You can always raise her status by raising her salary, and this will happen all round as soon as there is tax relief for childcare.

Nobody appreciates what I do

It is essential for everyone to feel that what they are doing is valuable and important. As the employer of a nanny, it is essential that you see yourself as an employer with a responsibility to develop the nanny to her full potential. This involves active awareness of the quality of her job, constant positive appraisal and often spoken expressions of thanks for a job well done. Be aware that her influence and values are having a positive effect on the children, and that her experience and training are a real and measurable factor that you openly appreciate.

Emergency cover

A good agent will have dependable emergency-cover people on tap for the sudden real emergency. 'The nanny has a temperature of 106 and I have to appear in court today. *Help!*' This is another reason why it is a good idea to develop a relationship with an agency. Over the years, the agency will get to know you and your family and will help you out of many a disaster. Develop your own extended family of friends who help each other out in emergencies. Don't leave the arrangements for helping each other out as a 'gentleman's agreement'. Organise with friends under clear-cut guidelines of who can do what for whom and how the favour is returned.

The nanny's responsibilities

A trained nanny expects to be responsible for everything related to her charges. She has been trained in all aspects of child development and, like a good general, is both prepared and waiting for the next challenge. She is there to stimulate the children in their next stage of development, mentally, physically and emotionally. This comes out in her day-to-day relationship with the children but she is aware of a greater purpose in the same way that caring parents are aware of a greater purpose.

Whose values?

Understanding and helping in the development of the child is the nanny's goal and purpose, and for her to take pride in her job she must get on with what she has been trained to believe is right. A nanny who is doing her job feels she is instilling certain values for life in areas of discipline and modes of behaviour. She may secretly feel that her values are somewhat counter to the parents' values, but unless you do, this is not a problem. Because a lot of working parents feel they are not with their children enough, they try to compensate materially with trips, presents and *spoiling*. This often leads to a three-year-old's firm conviction that everything is there for the asking, or perhaps demanding. The trained nanny believes she is there to counter this, and it's not such a bad thing. A good nanny wants to discuss often and thoroughly with her employers how they want their children to be brought up. Keeping in mind that she will still feel she is instilling her own values, never be too tired for a discussion.

Discipline

Nannies expect to discipline children but corporal punishment is rare. Norland's policy is that nannies don't smack children. However, a good nanny is a good disciplinarian. For children whose parents never discipline them, it is good to know where nanny stands. Parents who don't discipline will often allow the nanny to dispense discipline in front of them. Overstretched, tired parents often don't want to ruin the little time they have with their offspring and are grateful for the watchful eye of the nanny to behaviour that is not acceptable.

'Nanny, I don't feel well!'

The nanny is with your children all day. She is bound to know more about their state of health, when they last had a tummy ache and how they react to a scraped knee. In her training she will have worked not only in the local children's ward, but she will have some experience with disabled children. Her lexicon of medical terminology may be vastly superior to yours. When the doctor comes, don't be upset by the nanny having more inside information to give the doctor than you. She hasn't been withholding information. She has already told you everything she knows about the aches and pains, but often in front of the doctor her memory will be jogged for an extra helpful bit of information. Thank her for remembering. Don't be resentful that she only remembered it when she was confronted by the doctor. The doctor isn't making judgements; he just wants the facts.

If a child is sick in the night, a live-in nanny gets up. If it isn't serious, she probably won't wake you unless she feels it is necessary, if the child wants you or if the doctor needs to be called. If you always want to be woken when the child is ill, tell her.

A mother should be responsible for a child in the hospital and a nanny would think twice about working in a family where the mother didn't make time to be with the child in hospital. However, circumstances can make this impossible. Paediatric wards are concerned that someone with a meaningful relationship with the child is with him and will accept the presence of a close relative, a sibling or a nanny (see Chapter 11 on sick children).

The children's social life

The nanny will expect to arrange the children's social life. This is likely to revolve around the charges of other nannies. Expect this, as nannies befriend other nannies outside the school gates. If you are not in the crowd of faces waiting for the school to disgorge its charges, the nanny will talk and eventually form relationships with the faces she has something in common with, ie other nannies or mother's helps.

The partnership

Even if the nanny has sole charge of the children, the relationship between mother and nanny is still a partnership. It takes an experienced working mother not to feel both guilt and jealousy in large or small measure towards the nanny and her relationship with the children.

Is there any way to prepare yourself for these feelings? Think through your feelings and your relationship with her thoroughly. Don't sulk and feel resentful. Praise her for a job well done. In the same way that you would like to know immediately if your nanny is not happy about something, the nanny would also like to know if you would like her to do something differently. Smooth the way by exchanging concerns, defeats and success in the way you would with any partner.

Absorbing the job without instruction

This does not happen either in the office or in the home. You have to define clearly what the duties are, explain how no one can possibly remember everything and say, gently and clearly, that you will always say immediately if you don't approve of something, or if something makes you unhappy, and you would like her to do likewise. Mothers who have not stayed at home often have little idea of the time everything takes when accompanied by the demands of small children. At the office, each task is easily delineated, but this is not so in the home. You cannot programme the nanny and the children in the way you can programme and organise an office.

Holidays

Your holidays are not her holidays. She may find the excitement of a villa or hotel holiday great fun, but this should not detract from the fact that she is probably working twice as hard and longer hours while you have a rest. Her own holidays are a separate affair and should be anything from two to four weeks. Three is probably a good compromise. Like any other employee, her holidays are paid and this should be written into her contract.

'Oh my God, she's sick'

Everyone knows that mothers and nannies are never allowed to be ill, ever. Many employers are totally unsympathetic to a nanny who has a high temperature and is literally dragging herself around. Few families have a back-up system and beg the girl to pull herself together. 'Surely you can cope!' The last thing in the world anyone wants to do when they are feeling really rough is to carry on. A fairly young nanny who is used to curling up and being doted on by a loving mother when she is ill is going to feel doubly miserable if she is made to feel like a skiver because she caught little Jonny's flu. Be sympathetic and try to have a contingency plan.

The changeover of nannies

From the parent's point of view, a change can be a good thing. From the new nanny's point of view, children can become unstable if the major person in their lives is often changed. The child has had a real and important relationship with the nanny and the child must be given time to mourn the last nanny's departure and get used to the new one. Talk about it, explain why it is happening, and keep in touch with the old nanny for as long as necessary. You may find you keep in touch with her for ever.

Be aware of the following and you will have a happier nanny

Let's talk

Communication is particularly important and valuable regarding the needs of the children and the events of the day. A good nanny will want to fill in the day to the mother in the evening whether she is receptive or not. It is disheartening to a nanny to find that the mother is consistently exhausted and unreceptive. Many nannies have remarked that it often appears more difficult for the mother to turn off the office than for the father. Let the nanny in on why you might be so tired, ask her to give you time to wind down, and then *listen.*

Food, glorious food

Starvation rarely really happens and most nannies have a tendency to gain weight as anyone at home all day does. However, when both parents are often out to dinner, the nanny may find that there is no food in the house. Keep the larder well stocked and be considerate, fill it with non-fattening fare like apples, pears and crispbread.

Have you heard!

The grapevine works both ways and often the employer's grapevine gets back to the nanny and can be hurtful. Everyone talks about their nanny or au pair, but mean gossip or even a remark about the nanny's skin or weight can cause real pain. It's so easy to chat away about the nanny's defects and not her good qualities. Listen to yourself and, if you hear yourself saying things that you would not say to her, don't say them at all.

Hours of work

The most common complaint is that the job grows to fill the time available. If the nanny is a live-out nanny, when time is taken advantage of and the parents are consistently late coming home, her private life suffers. A live-in nanny often finds her time off is never real time off. This can cause great difficulties. It is so easy to ask for the nanny's help when she is available. If she comes down to make herself a cup of coffee, she lays herself open to a little request.

Privacy when off duty is important to the live-in nanny. She doesn't expect to have her lover come and stay the night but she does expect to be left alone.

Extra jobs that are not part of the nanny's responsibilities and eat into the girl's free time are a source of irritation. Don't ask her to clear up a mess not related to the children. If she is headed out the door to do a bit of shopping for herself, don't present her with your 40-item long Sainsbury's list with a 'Do you mind?'

Time ladies, please!

Curfews may allow the employers to rest easy that the nanny is not lying under the wheels of a number 10 bus but for the nanny, who is an adult, it is humiliating. In a good relationship, the nanny will let you know if she is going to be in late and will not make a habit of staying out terribly late as she will not be able to do her job properly. Your children will quickly tell you if she spends a good part of the day asleep.

Changing your plans

If you think you are going to change your plans, don't do so after the nanny has already changed hers. This could lead to murder. If you find you must change your plans, either try to do so well in advance, discuss the possibilities of changing the plans with her and then, if necessary, hire an alternative carer.

You were going to do that anyway, weren't you?

Exploitation, not only by the mother for whom she works but by other mothers, is a common complaint. For example, where there is a school rota and all the other drivers are mothers, often the mothers will ask the nanny to take over their driving time on the basis that she is a paid employee. These same women would not dream of phoning up another mother and saying, 'I have a dreadful headache, do you mind collecting the children today?'

Money

Nannies also complain of there not being a 'kitty' in the house for minor expenses. The family can often forget to reimburse for the milk bill or the egg delivery etc. Not being paid on time and having to ask for her money is a major and oft expressed complaint.

Financial responsibilities are part of the nanny's life as well as yours. If she lives out, she will be either paying off a mortgage or paying rent. She might have a dependent parent to whom she sends money, be buying a car, or saving for a holiday. Respect the fact that she needs to be paid regularly and reimbursed for any expenses.

Gross as opposed to net

Tax and National Insurance contributions must be paid as the nanny is an employee and you are her employer. Nannies understand their salaries on a 'clear' or 'all found' basis, but make sure that both you and the nanny understand what she is actually being paid. Her National Insurance contributions are paid both by you as her employer and by her, but if she only sees the all found sum, this may not impinge on her real understanding of what her salary is. Sit down with her, particularly if it is her first job, and explain to her carefully and thoroughly the value of her invisible pay. Let her know, in the nicest possible way, the sort of rent she would be paying for her accommodation whether you live in the Yorkshire Dales or Belgravia. Tell her about the cost of heating and food, hot water and the telephone, toilet paper and instant coffee. Compare the end result with the sort of spending money a secretary, paying her own tax and National Insurance contributions, rent and all the utility bills and feeding herself, would have at the end of the month. You are doing her a favour by making her aware, and a good understanding of home economics should bring a smile to her face. Always state her salary in terms of 'gross' and then explain how the 'net' amount comes about.

The lonely nanny

Leaving home can be the loneliest thing in the world for a young girl, in her first job without friends and with no one to confide in. Au pairs make friends of their classmates at language school. There is no such centre to a nanny's existence. On her first free weekend, she may be terrified to venture into town. She may not be interested in touring museums or walking alone in the countryside. A caring employer makes sure that for the first few weekends she is included in family activity or activity is organised for her. Homesickness coupled with friendlessness can turn a potentially excellent arrangement into a short-lived one if the problem isn't anticipated.

Before the girl arrives, contact friends with nannies and ask them to tell their nannies that your new nanny is about to arrive and you would like to take all the girls out to a film. You can't force friendships, but you can ease their development.

In 1981 a lonely but enterprising nanny named Loraine Thompson came to London and found the loneliness unbearable. Taking the bull by the horns, she put an advert in *Nursery World* for other nannies in the same predicament. Lots of girls replied to her advert and, as well as making friends, she identified a need. Now, back home in a job in South Shields, she has turned what she started as a hobby in London into a small business.

For a registration fee of £5 she will send you a list of other registered nannies in your area anywhere in the country. She has just bought a computer and is busy typing in names to make the process easier.

Nannies Need Nannies
Loraine Thompson, 28 May Street, South Shields, Tyne & Wear NE33 3AJ; 091-454 2617

The National Association of Certificated Nursery Nurses (NACNN) is a voluntary organisation for NNEBs which started in 1948. There are branches all over the country organising meetings for both social and educational purposes. It is possible for people working with the 0 to 7-year-olds to join as associate members without an NNEB certificate. Members attend the Annual General Meeting and participate in conferences and seminars. They send out a newsletter three times a year.

A nanny who contacts NACNN will be put in touch with her nearest branch members and encouraged to come to meetings. In this way, she will find an immediately available group of friends and the organisation is keen for nannies in residential work to participate.

Phyllis Mitchell
Secretary, National Association of Certificated Nursery Nurses, 10 Meriden Court, Great Clacton, Essex CO15 4XH; 0255 476707

The Professional Association of Nursery Nurses (PANN) is an independent trade union for nursery nurses, having received its certificate of independence in 1984 under the Labour Relations Act. PANN was formed in 1982 by a group of nursery nurses disturbed at the way some unions took industrial action which harmed children in their care and damaged relationships with the community. Members of PANN do not go on strike under any circumstances.

'PANN seeks to restore some of the professionalism which is in danger of being lost. It regards nursery nursing as a vocation with duties to the community and not simply a job done for a wage.' PANN is the only trade union nannies can join. It can represent a nanny in a residential situation but as yet does not have negotiating rights with local authorities.

Professional Association of Nursery Nurses (PANN)
St James Court, 77 Friar Gate, Derby DE1 1BT; 0332 43029

Chapter 7

Au Pairs

You can't cope and you need someone to make your domestic burden easier. Do you need a cleaning lady, a nanny, a mother's help or an au pair? A cleaning lady cleans the house but doesn't take care of the children. A nanny takes care of the children but does not do any housework. An au pair is a little bit of both but not all of both. A mother's help is more of both and more expensive. This chapter describes how to settle in an au pair, making the most of her presence in your home and her stay in Britain. Apply most of the advice regarding an au pair to a mother's help (see Chapter 8).

What is an au pair?

The current Immigration Rules describe the 'au pair' scheme as an 'arrangement under which an unmarried girl aged 17 to 27 inclusive and without dependants who is a national of a western European country including Malta, Cyprus and Turkey may come to the United Kingdom to learn the English language and to live for a time as a member of an English-speaking family.

A live-in au pair is expected to work approximately five hours a day or 30 hours per week doing light housework duties including care of the children. The current rate for an au pair is between £25 and £30 per week, depending on her responsibilities and she expects to have one full day a week free. An agency supplying an au pair expects anything up to a £60 placement fee, depending on the length of the placement. The great advantage of an au pair is that she is there, in the house, ready to help when you need her. She is not suitable for a family where both parents are out all day.

Twenty years ago, au pairs used to come from the middle and upper-midde classes. Nowadays, au pairs come from all sorts of family backgrounds. English is taught at all levels in school and its place as the universal language is understood by everyone. Social change and class mobility motivate any ambitious girl from any background to be an au pair for a year in Britain.

If you decide that an au pair is the most suitable solution to your domestic needs, the Home Office issues guidelines on who is eligible to become an au pair.

The Home Office and au pairs

The Home Office issues a leaflet, RON 2 (AP), which outlines the position of European Community nationals, non-EC nationals and Commonwealth members. An au pair who is a national of a country which is not in the Commonwealth or European Community must register with the police if she is going to stay longer than six months. Nationals of EC countries are allowed to take jobs in Britain, so her residency is not a problem. However, if she wants to stay longer than six months, she should apply for a residency permit. The leaflet also lists agencies which will help an au pair who is in difficulty and agencies which will help au pair girls find host families and vice versa. The Home Office has a London telephone number for recorded information on who is eligible to be an au pair and how long she can stay in the country: 01-760 1666. Citizens' Advice Bureaux can give advice on the legal and immigration status of au pairs.

Agencies and sources of information

An au pair agency is an employment agency like any other and must be licensed by the Employment Agency Licensing Office which is part of the Department of Employment, see page 71.

The Home Office leaflet, RON 2 (AP), lists a number of agencies which provide help in finding au pairs for families. One is the Federation of Recruitment and Employment Services Ltd, a voluntary body that publishes a list of licensed au pair agencies all over the country. Since it is a voluntary federation, and agencies must pay a fee to be on its list, not all licensed agencies are listed.

The Federation of Recruitment and Employment Services Ltd (FRES) 36–38 Mortimer Street, London W1N 7RB; 01-323 4300

The British Council issues guidelines regarding the Immigration Rules revised by Parliament with effect from 16 February 1983 as to who is eligible to become an au pair, her duties as an au pair and recommended pocket money. The British Council will send on request a list of organisations which will help girls who need advice once they have arrived in the UK, such as the Austrian Catholic

Centre or the YWCA, and will include a list of agencies from the FRES. However, the Council takes no responsibility, nor does it recommend these agencies.

The British Council
10 Spring Gardens, London SW1A 2BN; 01-930 8466

All local councils run Community Advice Bureaux which will provide either the names of agencies themselves or the name of an organisation that will supply a listing. There are about 825 in the UK.

Why a specialist au pair agency?

Many mothers feel that they would not want to hire an au pair without having interviewed her in person first. Interviewing an au pair who is already in the country can defeat your objectives for a long-term stay. A girl who is already in the country may have left another family and may not have come to Britain with the clear intent of adjusting to living with one family and studying English for a year. She will be less interested in being part of the family, having already made her own set of friends. She is unlikely to have the same commitment as a girl who has come to Britain expressly to study English.

The au pair you hire from an agency which arranges for girls to come from abroad knows she has to adjust to a strange country and a strange family and get on with her studies. If she is unable to make the adjustment or doesn't fit into the family, the agency will replace her. It is also difficult interviewing a potential au pair whose grasp of English is still fairly remote.

What a good au pair agency will do

A good agency will interview the girl abroad in her native country and send you a description of the girl and her interests, including her level of education; her domestic abilities and experience, particularly with young children; details of her family, its size and her place in it; and her father's and mother's professions.

It is more sensible to use an agency rather than run your own advert or put a card in a language school. The agency is there to listen to you and to the girl if you have problems. If the arrangement is unsuccessful, a good agency will find you a new girl and the girl another family. You are assured that the girl has been vetted and is suitable in the first place to be an au pair. An agency can give you guidelines on hours of work and suitable payment.

Writing to the au pair

The agency will send you the name of the girl, her picture, and brief information about her as described on page 93. If you think she might be suitable, you then write to her, usually care of the agency's agent abroad, describing your family and her duties. Write at length, enclosing pictures of the house and family so the girl has a good idea of what you are like and what her duties are going to entail. Be sure to ask her to send you her address and telephone number so you can phone her directly.

The au pair should be able, on arrival, to furnish the immigration officer with her valid passport and a letter of invitation from her hostess giving full particulars of the family and household; the duties she will be expected to undertake; the pocket money she will receive and the amount of free time she will have for study and recreation.

Here is an example of a letter to a prospective au pair. It is full of the required information and also shows interest and concern for the girl. It is admittedly long, but saves many problems in the future.

---

5 November, 1989

Miss Janine Benoit
c/o Amies de la Jeune Fille
8 Bellevue
Zurich, Switzerland

Dear Janine,

I have just spoken to Mrs ——— of ——— Service who has told me that you would like to come to London as an au pair. I would like you to start as soon after the summer as possible, on 2 or 3 September.

First, I shall tell you about our family. My husband is 35 and a chartered accountant. I am 33 and a part-time English teacher at a local secondary school. We have two sons: James, 8, and Harry, 6, and a daughter, Anna, who is 4. We are a Christian family but we are not religious. Neither of us smokes so it is most important that you are a non-smoker. We have a pet cat called Nantucket. We all enjoy sports and like to go on long

---

walks in the country.

Our house is in north London with easy access to all that London has to offer. We are very close to parks and woods. We are ten minutes' walk to both the tube and the bus. There is a swimming pool within walking distance.

The house is a modernised, well-equipped typical London town house on four floors. There is a kitchen, a utility room, a dining room and a play room on the lower ground floor, a sitting room and study on the ground floor, the master bedroom and Anna's room on the first floor and the boys' bedroom and the au pair's bedroom on the second floor. The au pair's bedroom is a pretty, carpeted and comfortable room. The au pair shares a bathroom with the boys. We have a small but pretty garden.

Your responsibilities would be to be in the kitchen by 7.30 am to make the coffee and set the table for breakfast. I would like you to help the children get dressed and organised in the morning and walk them to school. They all go to the same school and it is close by. Anna comes home at noon and I would like you to collect her. In the morning, you would (varying from day to day) iron, hoover, dust, generally tidy and do housework. I am usually home by 1 pm. In the afternoon, you would be free to go to school. I would expect you home in the evening (5.30 pm) in time to help with the evening meal. I would like you to help with the preparation, set the table, and help clear up after dinner. Depending on how quickly you work, or how you arrange your housework duties, you should be finished in the morning. I would like you to stay in to baby-sit one evening a week, occasionally two. In any case, I keep a calendar in the kitchen on which I write all our appointments so you know which evenings you have to stay in.

During the week, we tend to have dinner at 6.30 and we like to eat together as a family in the dining room. This is a good opportunity for you to be with us and practise your English.

I do not entertain a great deal, but when I do, I would ask you to stay in and help with the serving etc. If I am entertaining a family, we would invite you to join us.

There are many language schools to choose from. The private schools are more expensive than the state schools. The state schools are heavily subsidised by the government and it is possible to take a part-time course of ten hours a week for as little as £60–£100 a term but the cost of travel to and from the school by underground could cost the same, depending on how far away it is. There is a good state school within walking distance of the house – it is about a half-hour walk – which is more expensive – about £112 a term for eight hours a week. There is a private school practically on our doorstep that is more expensive still. When you arrive, I will take you round to the various schools. It is not easy to find a place as there are so many people after places but I have never failed to find an au pair a place in a school yet.

I would offer you £25 a week pocket money.

I have had eight au pairs over the last eight years. I am sure you would like to speak to one or two of them to get an idea of what it is like to be an au pair. Bettina Studer from Tingen in Germany was our au pair the year before last. Her phone number is 49-1649-6497. Before Bettina, Jacqueline Roget from Switzerland was with us. You can contact her at 41-9562-8709.

I enclose a picture of all of us taken last summer in Scotland. There are many families nearby who also have au pairs, and you will have no difficulty making friends.

Let me know as soon as possible if you would like to be our au pair, when you are arriving and how. I look forward to hearing from you.

Yours sincerely,

When the girl replies, you will be amazed at the standard of English. Don't use this as a gauge of her linguistic abilities because she will have asked friends to help her. In her letter, she will accept your invitation to come to Britain as your au pair and tell you how and when she is arriving. It is up to you and your agency whether you pay her travel expenses but this is not commonly expected.

Her arrival

She will probably arrive at an airport some distance from where you live. It is not reasonable to let the girl flounder in a strange country, but in this day and age she has probably done some travelling on ski holidays etc and may have even been to Britain before on holiday. Decide which is more convenient for you: to meet her at the airport or at a central train station or bus depot. If the station is more convenient, write to her describing how she transfers from the plane to the train, tell her to phone you from the airport when she arrives, and explain how you will meet her at the railway station.

How to recognise the au pair

You have a picture of her and she has one of you but often this is not enough. Arrange to meet her at the platform exit and tell her you will be holding a card or a piece of paper with her name on it. In this way, you will be instantly recognisable to her. It is a good idea to bring the children with you. They can hold the card with her name on it and they break the ice.

Meeting and greeting her

You want to set the right tone from the outset. Be friendly and welcoming but remember that you have invited the au pair to Britain to make your life easier and not the other way round. An au pair has a unique relationship with the family. She is not a guest in the house, she is certainly not a lodger, but she is also not quite a member of the family. You want to create a relationship where she is both able and used to taking instructions from you, happily, in the line of her responsibilities. Therefore, when you greet her, do not immediately relieve her of all her bags and start waiting on her hand and foot. Let her carry her bags with the children's help. Put her in the back seat of the car with the children so they can put her at ease on the way home.

Getting home and first impressions

The house

Her first impression of the house should be the way you want the house to be. This is entirely up to you but the girl's first impression of the house will tell her about the happily disordered or manically ordered way you want to live.

The au pair's bedroom

Her bedroom is where you want her to relax during most of her time off to give both you and her some privacy. If the room lacks any of the comforts of a bedroom one would wish to sit or read in, you will find her sitting at the kitchen table staring at your every movement. You can't tell her to go away if there is nowhere nice for her to go. Don't have different standards for yourself and for her. She will have come from a comfortable home and an attractive room. If you fill the room with all the family junk, she will not feel cosy, happy and contented, but homesick.

Her bedroom should have the following amenities:

- It should be carpeted, heated, warm and cosy.
- It should contain a desk, desk lamp and chair.
- Large pillows on the bed and adequate lighting should allow her to read on the bed.
- It should have enough wardrobe and shelf space for her clothes and books.
- A radio-cassette player is essential. A hair drier is a nice extra.
- The door should have a key so the au pair can lock it if she wants to, when she is in it and when she is not in it.

First job – first 'employee'

Most au pairs, unless they are very young, will already have had some sort of vacation or apprenticeship job. However, the situation of the au pair living with the family is unique. Her position in the family is difficult to define and you must do the defining immediately. You may never have had the experience of employing anyone before and be unused to organising someone else's responsibilities. But your ability to organise the au pair's day, imparting directives, criticism and, most important, praise to get the best attitude and performance from the au pair is the crucial factor in a successful relationship.

Guidelines for the day of arrival

Don't leave her floundering when she first arrives. After having been shown her room, she won't know what to do. Make her a cup of tea, tell her to unpack, clear the children out of the room so she has some privacy, and point out the daily routine chart you have put up on her wall. (see page 102). After an hour, knock on her door to make sure everything is all right, and tell her, when she is ready, to join you in the kitchen.

Give her a chore immediately. If her first impression is of coming into the kitchen and watching you work, this is what she will expect in the future. Arrange the first evening meal so that she helps with the preparation, laying the table and clearing away. Do not approach the first day with the idea that she must be tired and you will do everything for her. This sets the wrong tone for the relationship you want to establish. Unless she has arrived on an overnight flight from the Philippines, or by boat from Finland, a young girl is not going to be exhaused by a short trip.

Homesickness

It is a rare girl who doesn't feel some homesickness. Knock on her door on the first night after she has gone to her room, smile and tell her you are happy she is here and you are sure she will be happy with you. It is a kindness to let the girl phone home after she has arrived to tell her parents that she has arrived safely. Make sure she understands that this is special, and she is not allowed to use the phone to make long distance calls to her parents as a norm. Some girls are very homesick; some are not homesick at all. Keep asking her every few days if she still feels homesick. Eventually, she will find the question funny. Then you can stop.

The lonely au pair

Alone, away from your family, perhaps for the first time, in a foreign country where no one understands you is pretty hard to cope with at 18. The agency through which you found her will put her in touch with other girls in your area they have brought over. Some agencies arrange coffee mornings for the girls as a gesture of welcome and an aid to adjustment. Mrs Margrit Lyster, a social worker for the Swiss Welfare Office for Young People in London, has been counselling girls and mediating with agencies and families for 20 years. The Swiss Welfare Office is not an agency, but works with agencies, financed by the Swiss government to ensure that girls don't find themselves stranded and alone in London.

Swiss Welfare Office
31 Conway Street, London W1P 5HL; 01-387 3608

The Swiss Youth Club organises activities throughout the year for Swiss au pairs and welcome friends of members who are not Swiss.

Swiss Club
79 Endell Street, London WC2 1AJ;
01-836 1418 (Sunday evenings from 6.30 pm)
Contact: Mrs Monika Saes, Youth Worker; 01-340 9740
            Reverend Philippe von Orelli, The Vicarage, 1 Womersley
            Road, London N8 9AE; 01-340 9740

The Germans also have a youth centre which welcomes au pairs:

German Verein für Internationale Jugendarbeit
39 Craven Road, London W2 3BX; 01-723 0216

as well as the German Catholic Social Centre
Lioba House, 40 Exeter Road, London NW2 4SB; 01-452 8566

Several times a year, representatives from both German centres go down to the south coast and hold events for au pairs in the Bournemouth area. The Bournemouth contact for German au pairs is:

Mrs Hedy Rose
23 Richmond Park Avenue, Bournemouth; 0202 532600

There is a contact point for almost every nationality. Here are some useful addresses:

Austrian Catholic Centre
29 Brook Green, London W6 7BL; 01-603 2697

Austrian Social Services
18 Belgrave Mews West, London SW1X 8HU; 01-235 3731

Croatian Catholic Mission
17 Boutflower Road, London SW11 1RE; 01-223 3530

Danish YWCA
43 Maresfield Gardens, London NW3 5TF; 01-435 2007

Dutch Church
Austin Friars, London EC2N 2EJ; 01-588 1684

French Centre Charles Peguy
16 Leicester Square, London WC2H 7LP; 01-437 8339

French Hostel
61–69 Chepstow Place, London W2 4TR; 01-221 8134

International Catholic Society for Girls
ACISJF
24 Great Chapel Street, London W1 3AS; 01-734 2156

Italian Hostel
2 Chiswick Lane, London W4 2JF; 01-994 4951

Norwegian YWCA
52 Holland Park, London W11 3RS; 01-727 9346

Portuguese Community Centre
7 Thorpe Close, London W10 5XL; 01-969 3890

Spanish Hostel
189 Gloucester Place, London NW1 6VU; 01-723 1919

Spanish Hostel
38–39 Kensington Square, London W8 5HP; 01-937 5237

Swedish Church
6 Harcourt Street, London W1H 2BD; 01-723 5681

Finding a school

There is a wide variety of schools which offer full and part-time courses in English as a Foreign Language (EFL). Find out from your local authority what sort of classes are offered by its colleges and institutions of further education. You may find that English as a Second Language (ESL) only is on offer. There is not a great deal of difference and you may find this is wholly suitable for your au pair. ESL is aimed at immigrants and so the emphasis on what is learned is different, the classes being geared to a curriculum that helps the new immigrants to settle in Britain. ESL classes are attended in general by immigrants, whereas EFL classes are for foreign students. Your au pair is more likely to meet fellow au pairs and make friends in an EFL class.

In London the Inner London Education Authority has hitherto issued a booklet listing full-time, part-time and evening classes called English Classes for Students from Abroad. After 31 March 1990, when the ILEA is to be disbanded, EFL courses will be available from the individual education departments of each London borough and they will probably publish their own individual information.

ARELS-FELCO, The Federation of English Language Course Organisation, issues a booklet listing English Language courses all over Britain recognised by the British Council. Their booklet is available from:

ARELS-FELCO
2 Pontypool Place, Valentine Place, London SE1 8QF; 01-242 3136

Daily routine and duties

A daily routine chart should be pinned to a bulletin board or on the wall or wardrobe door in her bedroom for the girl to see immediately. Have three copies of this chart: one for her bedroom and one for each of you to carry round the house on the first full day while you explain it. Go through each item, one at a time so she understands exactly what she has to do. In the beginning, she will probably forget both to do the tasks and to look at the chart, but this is a start.

Here is an example of a daily routine chart.

Always lock your windows and security gate before you go out.

Always make sure all windows and doors are locked if you leave the house when no one else is at home.

Always tell me immediately if an appliance isn't working.

Always tell me immediately if you break something by mistake.

Daily duties

Morning

7.00   Wake up – put kettle on.
7.15   Make coffee.

First thing every morning:

Tidy cushions on living room sofa.
Tidy kitchen after breakfast.
Sweep leaves from front entrance to house.
Bring milk in.

Regular duties

8.45   Walk children to school.
12.00   Collect Anna from nursery school.

Vacuum two or three times a week or when necessary. Always check vacuum cleaner bag to make sure it does not need changing.

Polish brass on front door twice a week.

Iron when necessary.

Dust everywhere two or three times a week including lamps. Dust silver with a silver cloth. Use beeswax polish on antique furniture. Never spray directly on the piano.

Clean and polish sinks and mirrors and glass tables two or three times a week. When you polish glass, don't forget TV screens.

Always empty the dishwasher when the cycle is finished.

Look at 'write on – wipe off' board in kitchen for extra things.

Evening duties

Peel potatoes, make salad.
Set dining room table.
After dinner boys clear table, load dishwasher and tidy kitchen.

Before bed

Put cereals, bowls, spoons on kitchen table.
Put out empty milk bottles and milk order for next day.

Write on – wipe off board

As a supplement to the list in her bedroom, keep a chalk board or a write on – wipe off board in the kitchen for special chores not on her list, such as polishing silver. She can do these chores at her own pace and tick them off when she has done them. Have her tick them off, not wipe them off so you see what it was you asked her to do. It is easy to forget and ask her to do the same thing again immediately after she has done it.

Emergency numbers

In a prominent place in the kitchen, put up a notice instructing the au pair step by step how to make a 999 call, and whom to contact in case of emergency.

It should read as follows:

<u>EMERGENCY</u>

<u>DIAL 999</u>

A voice will ask: Police – Fire – or Ambulance

Say which one; then say our address: 12 Wood Ridge, London N6

Mr Davison's office number:	<u>888 1111</u>
Mrs Davison's school number:	<u>444 2222</u>
Our doctor: Dr John Wellbody:	<u>348 9999</u>
Our neighbours: Mrs Jones:	<u>341 5555</u>
Mrs Smith:	<u>341 6666</u>
Mrs David:	<u>340 1221</u>

The dishwasher

If the girl has never used a dishwasher before, it is vitally important to show her carefully how to load the machine without obstructing the spray arms. If she doesn't understand this, it will cost you a lot of money. Inspect how she loads the machine until you are entirely satisfied that she can load it competently before you let her turn it on by herself.

The dishwasher test is an infallible gauge of the grey matter at work. After explaining how a dishwasher works, if you find that she then puts the glasses in upside down, it will be clear to you that she is going to need a lot of general instruction.

The vacuum cleaner

It is a rare au pair who notices when the vacuum cleaner bag is full. Unless the au pair is amazingly conscientious, check this yourself.

The washing machine and drier

The same applies to the drier. Check and clean the filter yourself. If the au pair does all the laundry, washing as well as ironing, discipline her carefully as to the size of load the washing machine can accommodate and how to separate the laundry into different temperature washes. A stray red sock can have a disastrous effect on a load of 'whites'. Repairs are expensive if she overfills the machine, and running costs are expensive if she uses the machine to wash two pairs of her knickers. In the end, it might prove easier and more efficient to load the machine yourself.

Laundry – the au pair's and the family's

It is important to organise how the au pair's laundry will be done as soon as the girl arrives. If you want her to do her own laundry, you will have to trust her to use the machine herself, which can prove expensive in the long run. If you do all the washing together and want her to add her laundry to the family wash, put a laundry basket in her bedroom for her dirty clothes and tell her that you will let her know when you are going to do the laundry. Once you have separated the family clothes into different temperature washes, tell the au pair to add her clothes to the piles. Most young girls want their clothes washed a great deal more often than is really necessary. It is simpler to indulge this than to hand her something back that she has worn once and put in the laundry. She will probably hand wash her undergarments. Make sure she knows where to hang dripping hand washing.

Pocket money

Au pairs working not more than 32 hours per week and baby-sitting not more than three evenings should receive pocket money of around £25 per week. If the girl is expected to prepare evening meals by herself, drive the children around etc, the maximum amount of pocket money should be paid. It is up to you whether you pay the girl's travelling expenses, and/or her English lessons but this is not generally expected. For girls from wealthy countries, the pocket money might seem a small sum, and they might feel underpaid. The au pair will compare her situation with her fellow au pairs as regards both duties and pocket money. This may make her appreciate her situation; it can also make her feel hard done by. If the girl has never had a job before, and particularly has never lived away from home before, she will have no concept of the pocket money as 'all found' income, and may feel underpaid. It is worth spending time explaining this to her. Tell her that you hope she understands that the £25 is only pocket money and what she is really being paid is the room of her own, food, laundry, use of the phone, heating, and all the comforts of home. If she has never had to pay for these benefits, she will find this difficult to comprehend. You might add that a student would pay £80, or whatever the going rate in your area is, to live in that room with all found.

Your au pair depends on her pocket money for expenses. If you go away for a week and leave her in the house, she still has the same expenses and it really isn't fair to give her less than her normal rate when you are not there. She is house-sitting and you can leave a list of chores to be done while you are away.

What she wears in the house

What do you do if she appears in fluffy bedroom slippers and huge quilted housecoat, and still is clad in this ensemble at 11 am? You may not mind, but it isn't very professional or disciplined. On the other hand, you may mind but you may like to remain similarly clad yourself until late morning. It is tricky to look at someone in a dressing-gown while you are wearing one and ask her to get dressed. However, if you have put 'Get dressed' on the routine chart, you can tactfully ask the girl to comply.

Understanding and assessing the girl

In every stereotype there is a grain of truth.

Nationality. There is no way round it, different nationalities do have differing personalities. A German girl will probably work faster and be more organised than a Spanish girl. A Swiss German girl will probably leave everyone else standing with her speed and organisational ability. A Spanish girl may be cuddlier than a French girl who may be cuddlier than the efficient Swiss girl, or perhaps the other way round. A girl might seem opinionated because this is part of her culture, but in fact be rather unsure of herself. She might work slowly, also a national characteristic, but be efficient in the long run. Don't pre-judge a girl by her national stereotype, but allow for and be tolerant of national characteristics.

Finding a balance – a compromise

No one is good at everything. The girl who is sensationally efficient at keeping the house in order may not be warm and loving towards the children. The qualities that allow someone to sit and play patiently for hours with a three-year-old are different qualities from those that propel the girl to have all the laundry done immaculately by 8.30 am. Rarely are all qualities found in the same person. One au pair will be wonderful with the house; the next one will be wonderful with the children. The trick is to accept each girl on her own terms and make the most of her.

Intelligence

It doesn't take long to assess the general intelligence level of a new au pair. However, there are different kinds of intelligence and it is important that the girl is never made to feel stupid. Some girls will take a long time before they remember to do everything, even with a list pinned to their bedroom wall. Others will be totally capable of running your house within a fortnight. If she is slow to remember, tell her that you understand that there is far too much to remember, and gently remind her. Losing your patience, and then your temper with a girl who is slow or forgetful will only exacerbate the situation by making her feel inadequate. From her point of view, she is unable to defend herself because of her limited ability to express herself in English.

Telling an au pair the obvious

'But it's obvious; surely I don't have to tell her to wash the potatoes before she cooks them.' Her mother may have taught her that potatoes taste better if cooked in their own mud. Nothing is obvious from one culture to another. Never shy away from explaining or requesting 'the obvious'. It is only obvious to you, not to her.

Settling in

It always takes at least twice as long to do almost everything than you initially estimated, and this includes housework. It is a good idea to time yourself doing household tasks so you have some idea how long it should take; for example, to vacuum the whole house from top to bottom. Then take into account that you can do it faster than anyone else. Don't expect the au pair to do things you couldn't do, or work at a speed no one could possibly work at. It is not possible to look after a baby, prepare lunch and dust and vacuum the house in the two hours you are gone.

Remember what it is like to be 18

Most 18-year-olds are pretty bound up in themselves. If you understand that, and remember what you were like when you were 18, you will develop a good relationship with her. Her experience is limited. She is still close to being a child herself. Take advantage of this fact: she might sometimes have greater insight into children, to whom she is closer in age, than you.

Don't allow the children to invade her room at will, and don't invade it yourself. Make sure the children understand that the room is off limits to them. Always knock before you enter.

Always speak English

If you can speak her native language and you are worried that she has not understood, for the first few weeks you might repeat what you have said in her native tongue. However, she is in the UK to learn to speak English, and not for you to brush up your French or German or whatever. It is unfair for the host family to speak to the au pair in her native tongue as this defeats the entire purpose of her being in Britain.

Praising and complaining

It is always easier to blame than praise. After she has been with you a few days, visit her in her room and ask her if she is happy and settled, if her feelings of homesickness have gone, and if everything is all right. After you have discussed her worries, you can talk to her about being an au pair, tell her how pleased you are with her and then discuss things that you might like done differently.

Staying right

The ever-rising spiral of expectations

You want her to start out happily, so you take her to a West End musical and two movies in the first week. This is a terrible mistake. First, she will come to expect this as a way of life and expect to go with you whenever you go out or take the family out. Second, it is not the norm of how you live. Since you want her to understand as quickly as possible what her role is in relationship to you, what you expect of her and what she should expect of you, start the way you want to continue. It isn't necessary to include her in every family outing, but it is welcoming for her if she is invited to join in at the beginning of her stay. She will quickly make her own friends at the language school and prefer going off with them. She should not be left in the house lonely and alone on her first Sunday with you.

The ever-rising spiral of work

Don't take advantage of a girl who works faster than average and therefore seems to have a lot of time to spare or of a girl who works efficiently. For example, if she does the ironing in her room in the evening, she will have, as a result, a lot of time to herself during the day. Don't fill that time up with more work for her to do. Measure the amount of work the girl does, within reason, by tasks and not by time. If a girl has hidden talents that are useful to the family, don't exploit them unfairly. For example, if the girl reveals herself as a gourmet cook, she should not suddenly find herself cooking all the meals.

Accident aware and accident prone

Being able to understand and identify cause and effect is an important indicator of intelligence. There are basic rules for safety in the kitchen and home which, if not followed, may lead to accidents. If they relate to the safety of children, the au pair will be unused to them unless she has a young sibling and she will have to be reminded.

Here are some examples of these rules:

1. Always turn a pot or pan handle in so it cannot be reached by a small child.
2. Always load sharp knives in the dishwasher blade side down. A toddler could potentially fall on to the cutlery rack and seriously cut himself.
3. Never put a pot of tea where a child can reach it. Never put the kettle where a child can reach it. Don't hold the baby in one hand and a boiling cup of tea in the other.
4. Never leave a baby unattended on the changing table.
5. Always relatch the stair gates.
6. Never leave a child unattended in the bath.
7. Always put cold water into the bath first, then hot.

All the above are common sense if the children are your own but not to an au pair who is unused to small children. Remind her and remind her until she doesn't forget.

Accident prone people tend to be unable to relate cause and effect. You have only one baby and you don't want him to be at risk under any circumstances. Constantly feeling worried because you doubt the girl's ability to react appropriately in situations of danger, or simply in traffic or the playground, is neither acceptable nor bearable. If, for example, you find the new au pair draws the bath, puts your small baby in it and comes down to make herself a cup of tea, you have got someone who doesn't recognise or understand the risk of accident. I would advise you to call the agency and suggest this girl would be better suited to a family with older children. You have only one baby. There are lots of au pairs in the world.

Playing fair

Dinner time

Dinner time, if the family sits down together, is when the au pair is most obviously part of the family. At first, she will be reluctant to join in the conversation because her English isn't good enough and she can't, and also because she will probably be a little shy. As her English improves, she will start to participate more and more. Strike a balance between talking to the children and talking to the au pair, making sure no one feels left out.

When she is eating dinner with the family, do not expect her to clear the table while the family remains seated. It makes her feel like a servant which she isn't. Get the children to help her clear the table.

If you want to eat alone with your husband one evening, explain this to her and prepare her dinner on a tray for a TV dinner. It is not comfortable for her to sit in on a quiet dinner for two and she will probably be only too glad to have a TV dinner.

If your children are very small and you don't have dinner together as a family, it is often more comfortable and agreeable for the au pair to eat with the children but you must be careful that she is not being fed a diet consisting entirely of nursery fare.

If she stays at home on her day off, ask her if she wants to be included in meals and explain to her that if she joins you for dinner she must help. If she wants to eat with you, she will be delighted to help. It is important for the girl that you don't make her feel like part of the family during the week and an intruder on her day off.

Baby-sitting – evenings in and out

Keep a calendar where everyone can see it in the kitchen. Explain to the girl that when you need her to be at home to baby-sit, you will write in 'Janine [au pair's name] in'. Tell her that when she wants to make arrangements to go out in the evening she must ask you first if it is all right, and then write in the calendar 'Janine out'. This way you will never be in the dreadful position of having told the au pair she can go out, and suddenly realising that you need her to stay in. Also, the au pair can see in advance which evenings she is needed to baby-sit and can plan accordingly.

Her holidays

The au pair should have bank holidays off or be compensated for them by having other days off. Otherwise, she will feel it is unfair if everyone else is on holiday and she has to work. She may ask you if she can take holidays while she is staying with you; for example, she may want to go home for a week to ski in the winter. Whether you allow her to do this is entirely up to you. Most girls will want to go home at Christmas for two weeks. If she doesn't, she should be included in all the Christmas festivities. New Year's Eve can cause problems as she may want to go out too. You have to work this out between you, but keep in mind that you are the boss.

Your holidays

You may want the au pair to come with you on your holiday. If you leave her at home, house-sitting, it is a nice perk to ask her if she would like to invite her parents to come and stay with her. If she does this, make your own decision as to whether you give her pocket money for the time you are away. If her parents come, she won't have the same expenses because her parents will be providing for her and you are providing them with a free holiday.

Her birthday

Make sure you ask her when her birthday is when she arrives, mark it on the calendar, and be sure to celebrate the day with a cake and a card. Celebrating your birthday away from home is a lonely event the first time it happens, particularly if nobody else knows about it. Children love birthdays, so it is not difficult to turn the au pair's birthday into a happy family event.

The au pair's day off

The au pair's day off must be a genuine day off, even if she spends it in the house. It is unfair if you leave everything on her day off for her to do the next day. If she is in the house, do not make her feel unwelcome. You may look forward to the day when she is not in the house, but if she is made to feel like an intruder, you increase her sense of isolation.

Some au pairs will make friends immediately and always have something to do when they are not 'on duty'. Other girls might be shy or have less imagination and find it difficult to make friends and find ways of amusing themselves. When the girl first arrives, try to help her with things to do by giving her literature on local points of interest and activities. Introduce her to the au pairs of friends as soon after she arrives as possible. Never force a friendship upon her, but give her the opportunity to meet other au pairs whose company she might enjoy.

Leching husbands – provocative au pairs

Which came first, the chicken or the egg? You know what your husband is like. If you know your husband has a roving eye, this can be a serious problem. However, it is you and your husband's problem and not the au pair's. The au pair may or may not be sexually experienced, but unless she indulges in overtly flirtatious behaviour, she is a captive in your home and must be protected. If she gives the impression of going out of her way to attract the attention of your husband in anything other than an innocent way, the situation must be resolved to put your mind at ease. You will have to look inside yourself as to whether you know yourself to be a naturally jealous person. It may all be in your imagination. On the other hand, it may not. The first person to talk about it to is your husband.

Depending on the culture of the girl, au pairs display differing degrees of personal modesty. An Italian or Spanish girl will generally be a great deal more physically modest than a Swedish girl. A young liberated girl of the 1980s may also be firmly of the belief that a sexual response to her behaviour is the man's problem and not hers. In the summer, she might wear a loose fitting T-shirt with nothing but her firm and voluptuous young breasts underneath. The poor husband is having to sit on his hands. This is a rather personal subject to broach with the girl. However, you must broach it because it is probably as disturbing to your husband as it is to you. The girl, in all likelihood, will have no idea. 'In Sweden everybody walks around topless at the beach. It is nothing.' Tell her it isn't nothing in Surbiton, or Chiswick, or wherever you live.

The au pair, on the other hand, may find herself subjected to sexual advances from the husband and father in the family that she has no knowledge of having provoked, and no idea how to deal with. The girl is in the invidious situation of either having to put up with unasked for attention or of giving offence. She may have developed a close relationship with you and be worried about upsetting you with the problem. In any case, she will be abysmally unhappy and probably ask to leave. If you discover that this is the reason, get rid of your husband and keep the au pair.

Personal hygiene

Some 18-year-olds want to spend all day in the bath tub. Others are only faintly familiar with its existence. The latter persuasion is rare among girls but it does exist. Cleaning toilets and bath tubs after use is an essential part of a child's training. Your au pair may not have been taught. If not, you will have to teach her.

1. If the girl smells, it could be her clothes. Check this when you put her clothes in the washing machine. If it is the girl herself, you will have to tell her to use a deodorant. Buy a deodorant for her yourself and approach her quietly in her room. Tell her that you are happy with her except for one small problem. Give her the deodorant as a gift, pick the prettiest one on the market, and tell her she really should use it. This is an intimate problem but one that must be dealt with. You cannot have the au pair leaving her bouquet in every room she is in.

2. Sanitary towels etc may cause a problem. Provide a little lidded waste basket next to the toilet she uses and tell her that it is for her used towels and that she should empty it herself into the dustbin.

3. If you find the toilet in a state, and you know it is the au pair who has used it, deal with it immediately. This is probably the most difficult situation to deal with directly. I have developed the following procedure. I clean the toilet myself and immediately afterwards tell the girl I have done so. Then I go on to say that I am just teaching the children to clean the toilet after themselves and they sometimes forget, but if she ever finds it dirty she is to tell me immediately so that I can make the guilty child clean it. I guarantee she will never leave the toilet dirty again. If your children are babies, this is not a possible approach and you will have to face the problem directly. 'Please be sure to clean the toilet after you have used it.'

February slump

This is an understandable reaction to the dreary greyness of a British winter and the tedium of housework, particularly if the girl started her year with you in September. It shows itself in the girl being tired and headachy, not very enthusiastic about doing things and wanting to sleep during the day. If you notice that your au pair is somewhat depressed mid-winter, talk to her about it, explain that it happens to everyone, and try to be jolly. Notice how she feels daily, and let her know that you understand and that you care about her.

Try to arrange treats for her and praise her work. Show her you *appreciate* her.

Food – hers, yours, and the children's

All au pairs gain weight. It is an unusual au pair who doesn't suddenly become diet conscious after a few months. In her attempts to solve this problem:

1. She will ask you if she need not eat dinner with you. This may have a double purpose: (a) her attempt to diet, and (b) a hidden wish not to have to clean up the kitchen in the evening.

Explain to her that the best way to lose weight is to eat proper meals, and what she should be giving up is the eating between meals. If she is unconvinced, assure her that even if she doesn't join the family for evening meals, she must still help with the preparation and clearing up afterwards.

2. She may go on strange diets of her own devising that interfere with your food planning for the week. For example, she may decide that an all-apple diet will solve her problems, or an all-tomato diet. You will suddenly discover that the tomatoes or apples that you bought on Monday, intending them to last the whole week, have disappeared by Wednesday. You must explain to her immediately that keeping the house supplied with food has to be planned and that you cannot restock something in the middle of the week because she has suddenly eaten it all. Tell her that if she wants to eat nothing but tomatoes, she will have to buy them herself. If the ingredients she uses to prepare something for herself don't matter, allow her to cook things for herself. It gives her a sense of independence.

3. She may eat the leftovers that you were planning to use for dinner. Don't be embarrassed about telling her to ask you first before she eats something. Food is always an embarrassing subject, particularly if the girl thinks she has a weight problem. Almost all

young girls are convinced they have a weight problem. You must tackle the subject at the beginning and perhaps help and advise her about dieting and her weight.

4. If she prepares food for the children, either instruct her what to make or observe what she does make for them and be sure it is something you approve of. If she comes from a food culture where carbohydrates and stodge are a main part of the diet, she may be plying the children with fattening fare of which you don't approve.

Family life and the au pair

Relationship with the family
What sort of relationship the girl has with the family is dependent on a number of factors: her age and independence; her maturity; the age of the children; and her own emotional needs. The older the girl is, the more quickly she will establish a life independent of the family. The older the children are, the less involved the girl will be in their lives, and hence the more independent. Girls are more likely than boys to want to develop a closeness with the au pair as they get older, so if you have only sons, the au pair is less likely to be a great part of their lives after they are nine to ten. Her own emotional and family needs will dictate whether she wants to cuddle the children when they watch after-school television or, if they are older, join them in listening to pop music.

Family arguments in front of the au pair
Don't involve the au pair in family squabbles. This is not only embarrassing but a great burden for the girl. A wife complaining about her husband to the au pair or a husband complaining about his wife involves the girl in your marital relationship, asks her to take sides and confuses her about her relationship with you both. If you feel a good fight coming on, delay it until you are alone, or go into another room. There is nothing worse than being the third party during a heated family row, particularly if you are a 17- or 18-year-old girl who is not really part of the family.

Responsibility for disciplining children
You will find that the degree of sympathy for, empathy with and understanding of children varies enormously from one au pair to another. This will soon become apparent in the relationship you

observe developing between the au pair and the children. Don't leave the girl to work this out entirely on her own, because the way she treats the children will have a temporary, if not a lasting, effect on them.

1. *Does she play favourites?* She may be partial to the baby and find the two-year-olds intolerable, which will just exacerbate the two-year-old's frustrations. Point this out to her. She will, in all probability, be surprised and try to adjust her behaviour.

2. *Does she tolerate too much/too little disorder with the children's toys?* If she is a particularly orderly au pair, she may tidy away the children's toys the minute they put them down, leaving them next to nothing to play with. On the other hand, she may allow them to get out every toy they possess and leave them scattered all over the place for days. A middle ground must be found that suits your own temperament.

3. *Does she expect too much of the children?* She may be telling your left-handed, glasses-wearing five-year-old that he must be stupid because he can't tie his own shoelaces. Try to be aware of this sort of thing by talking about the children's problems and difficulties with the au pair and by asking the children if they think the au pair understands them. If you confide in her that one of your children is having a particular problem, she will be much more sympathetic and understanding.

4. *Does she hit the children?* Do you hit the children? She will probably follow your lead on this. Whether you allow her to hit them is up to you but if you don't and she does, she probably comes from a culture where it is natural to slap children in order to discipline them. This also applies to yelling at them.

Most au pairs are not keen actively to discipline children, particularly older children. It is not always reasonable to expect a girl, who is close to being a child herself to be able to keep older children in order. The children themselves must be made to understand their relationship to her and not take advantage of it, and they should be scolded for doing so. Small children don't understand the different relationship this young girl has to them and their behaviour. If they find she is a push-over, they may be utterly appalling. The au pair must have some power to discipline. Otherwise her time with the children will be unbearable to her and she will not be happy. Talk to her about means of disciplining the children and come to certain agreements regarding slapping or spanking young children. If you disapprove of slapping children as a way of making them behave, tell her so immediately.

5. *Do the children play her off against you?* 'I'll tell Mummy you did that.' This is not a threat to cheer an au pair's heart. The children must be told by you that the au pair is boss when you are not around. If the girl knows that you have confidence in her ability to discipline and control the children, she will be much happier and contented in her relationship with them.

The au pair's maturity

The degree of maturity of the au pair will fundamentally affect her relationship to her responsibilities and to you and the children. Eighteen-year-old girls come in varying stages of maturity, from the extremely responsible and competent to the totally, irresponsibly incompetent. Provided the girl is not too irresponsible to be an au pair, you have to work with the girl herself and gauge your expectations on the degree of maturity you perceive. Discipline and maturity go hand in hand, and the less mature a girl is, the less disciplined she is going to be about her duties. If she leaves things until the last moment and then does them superficially, you will have to talk to her seriously about growing up and discipline. You do not want to spend the year searching for clothes in a pile of as yet unironed washing.

Her girl friends

If a friend comes to visit her in the house, where do they sit and what do they do? This can be disruptive to you and you must set down guidelines at the beginning. If you enjoy having the girls round the kitchen table, fine, but if you don't, ask her to entertain friends in her room when you are at home. Tell her she can make tea or coffee and then carry it up to her room on a tray. This gives her privacy as well.

Her boy friends

If she meets a young man in the local pub, she may want to bring him round to the house. It is up to you to set down strict rules and guidelines about inviting boys to the house, particularly when you are out and she is baby-sitting. You do not want anyone in the house who you do not approve of, and, although the young man may be nice, he may not be. He might spend an evening with your au pair casing the contents of the house for future reference.

If she develops a relationship with one boy, insist on meeting him. You are in this instance, and particularly if she is young, 'in loco parentis'. If he is a nice boy, he will be only too happy to meet you. You might find it is an added bonus to have a young man attentive to your au pair. She will be happy to have a boy friend; the children will enjoy a new person in their lives; and it is good practice for later when your own daughter(s) has/have boy friends.

Pop music

If you don't like pop music filling the house all day and she likes to listen to it, you can either tell her she is not allowed to play music while she works or buy a walkman for her use – a much friendlier solution.

Friends, neighbours and the au pair

Don't force your au pair to be a friend of your friend's au pair because it is convenient for you. The girls may not like each other and if you push too hard, it puts the girl in an embarrassing situation where she eventually has to say 'I don't like her'.

Neighbours may notice you have an au pair and see the girl as a potential baby-sitter for them. This somewhat defeats the purpose of your having an au pair as, if the girl is booked up weeks in advance with the neighbours, you can't go out spontaneously. Your au pair will want to earn the extra money baby-sitting once it is offered to her, so you must establish guidelines immediately, either saying that she cannot baby-sit for other families at all, or that she may but only, for example, one night a week. You have an au pair for your convenience, not for your neighbours', and you must make this abundantly clear to neighbours and friends from the beginning. If anyone asks your au pair to baby-sit for them without bothering to ask first if it is acceptable to you, I would explain to the au pair why this is unreasonable and ask her never to sit for that particular person. Your au pair may baby-sit on her night out without telling you. Provided she does not ask for an unreasonable number of evenings out, this is up to her.

Poaching the au pair

People are amazingly unscrupulous and au pairs, like nannies or dailies or cooks, are prey to the domestic poacher. You can neither avoid nor control this situation except by being a good friend to the girl and making sure lines of communication are always open. You cannot stop the grass from being greener somewhere else, but you can create a relationship of loyalty and caring that the girl would not want to leave. However, even the best laid groundwork can fail if a large enough enticement is dangled in front of your girl (a trip to America, for example). She will only be attractive to someone else if she is good. If she is stolen after you have spent months training her to be good, you will be annoyed, inconvenienced and hurt. There is nothing you can do save spread nasty rumours about the family she has gone to. Go ahead. It will make you feel better.

Leaving and remembering

If you have had a good relationship with the au pair, she will be sad to leave you and you will be sad to see her go. She will have become attached to the children and they will have become attached to her, girls more so than boys in many instances. But children can be heartless. Make sure you have briefed yours not to ignore her tearful departure and ask excitedly in the middle of a fond farewell where the next au pair comes from. Remember to send your previous au pairs Christmas cards and make the girl feel that she will always be welcome for a visit. You are probably the first experience she has had away from home, and the quality of that experience is important.

What have you gained by having an au pair?

Your stress level in running a house and family will have been greatly alleviated by the extra pair of hands. You have had to adjust to a stranger living in the house, and she has had to adjust to living in a strange house. If you have been able to make that adjustment and find that the presence of an au pair has been of benefit and not stress producing, it has been a successful arrangement. The children will not only have had the advantage of another adult available to them, but will have learned a little more about people and life by having to adjust to a girl from a different culture with different ways from their own. Her presence and the adjustments they have had to make should have enriched their lives and set them on the road to being Europeans in the twenty-first century.

The quality of relationship will vary from girl to girl. You will have a greater rapport with some girls than with others. Some you will remember and keep in touch with for ever, and some will disappear and never be heard from again. Every au pair will not be an equal success, but you will learn a little from each one, and with each new girl the relationship and the management will become easier.

Chapter 8

Mothers' Helps and Baby-Sitters

The mother's help

Mother's help is the term for a live-in girl who is not a trained nanny and not an au pair but who is employed by a family to help with both the children and the domestic chores. Her duties are far more broad than those of a qualified NNEB and her hours much longer than an au pair's. A mother's help works a nanny's hours with the sort of responsibilities of an au pair. She must be over 17, and is judged on her personal qualities and experience. Seventeen covers a multitude of sins in degrees of maturity. The guidelines described in dealing with the development and 'growing up' of an au pair should be applied equally to a mother's help (see Chapter 7).

Who are mother's helps?

Being a mother's help is a good discipline for a girl without any clear idea of what she wants to do and without any specific skills that would lead her to office work. Parents of school-leavers are often pleased to see their daughters entering a disciplined job environment that is also caring and personal and will give their child a broader view of the outside world. The girl might have a few O levels or GCSEs and be in the process of making up her mind about what she ultimately wants to do. As a youngster, she has probably had a lot of experience caring for siblings and baby-sitting, enjoyed the work and is finding out if she wants to make a career of it.

Most mother's helps are all too happy to collude with their employer, calling themselves 'nanny' from day one. This is rather hard on the real nanny as it negates her professional aspirations.

Work permits

Travelling Canadians, Australians and New Zealanders often work as mother's helps for a short stint during their travels. This can develop into a long stint if they like the family and the job. Commonwealth nationals can stay for up to two years under the

Working Holiday-Makers Scheme which is part of the Immigration Act of 1971. Under the terms of the scheme, the work should be part time and incidental to the holiday and the young people must be between the ages of 18 and 28. After two years, they are expected to return to their own country.

Non-EC and non-Commonwealth nationals need a work permit. It is illegal under the Immigration Act of 1971 to work without one and a family employing a foreign national without a work permit can be fined anything up to £2000. For further information contact:

The British Home Office for Immigration
40 Wellesley Road, Croydon, Surrey CR9 2BY; 01-686 0688.

Not doing things according to the rules is always terrific until something goes wrong. Something always goes wrong. The work permit *does* matter.

How to find a mother's help
Look for a mother's help in the same way that you would look for a nanny. Either place an advertisement in *The Lady*, *Nursery World* etc, or go through an agency. Occasionally, a girl advertises for a job herself.

Pay and taxes
A mother's help would expect to be paid from £65 to £100 gross per week in the same way that a nanny is paid. Her tax and NI contributions should be arranged in the same way a nanny's are. The salary and payment conditions are no different except for the fact that a mother's help is paid less because she is untrained.

The interview
Apply the same principles as you would to interviewing a nanny and make sure you get references (see pages 78–9).

What to expect of a mother's help
Unlike a nanny, who has a clear idea of what her duties and responsibilities are, there is no clear and absolute job description for a mother's help. What she is expected to do depends entirely on the individual arrangement with the family. The interview is, therefore, important for defining exactly what the mother's help's duties and responsibilities are going to be as well as her hours of work. Many

families prefer the mother's help because she is more malleable, will muck in and is happy to work either alongside the mother or alone doing whatever is necessary to keep the household ticking over.

She is expected to 'muck in' with everything, helping with the children and the housework. Her degree of maturity will determine how she handles herself. The effect of her cumulative experience as a mother's help will reveal itself soon enough in her reliability, confidence and ability to cope. You should expect the agency to have vetted a girl who is beginning as a mother's help carefully.

Nowadays, it is virtually essential for a mother's help to be a driver and it is difficult to place a girl who cannot drive.

Whose standards?

Mother's helps, like au pairs, come from every sort of class and economic background. How do you tell a girl from the same culture that she doesn't understand the meaning of 'clean'? With very great difficulty, is the answer. You can't subtly tell her that 'we' do it differently, because she is 'we'. However, you must tell her and you must tell her at the beginning. She may have grown up in a household where the frying pans were never washed or the hob unit never wiped. If she swears she has already wiped a surface and you are both staring at a patina of grease which she neither sees nor recognises, you must attack the problem head-on. Get out the sponge, put on the rubber gloves, pour on the cleaner and show her. If you don't, in very short order the entire house and everything in it will be covered with that same patina of grease. She may decide that you are a truly crazed cleanliness fanatic. Who cares! At least your house will be kept at your standards.

Baby-sitters

Baby-sitting has traditionally been the way teenage girls earn pocket money. Teenage boys have long since noticed that baby-sitting is usually an easy way of earning extra pocket money and so it is not difficult to draw on the services of local adolescents, male and female, to sit with the children while you go out in the evening. Baby-sitters have got younger and younger and it is not uncommon to find 13-year-olds prepared to spend the evening in your living room, being paid to watch the television while you go to the theatre. It is alarming to open the door to the new and recommended baby-sitter to find her barely older than the children of whom she is supposed to be in charge. In fact, according to the Children and

Young Persons Act, a baby-sitter employed to be in charge of young children in your home should be 16 or older.

The maturity of adolescents varies enormously as do the experience and confidence they possess in being in charge and caring for young children, especially babies. It is often reassuring to use the teenage son or daughter of a local family you know. The knowledge that, if there were serious problems and you were not easily contactable, the parents of the sitter would be available to give advice over the phone or even come round to help is reassuring. In the final analysis, you must be the judge of whether a teenager is mature enough to baby-sit for you.

Adolescent baby-sitters rarely do more than play a little bit with older children, tell them when to go to bed and make sure they stay there. An older sitter won't clear away the dinner dishes or do the ironing unless you have a special arrangement with her and pay her extra for doing do. The rates for baby-sitting vary enormously depending on the age and experience of the sitter and the area in which you live. You pay the going rate for your own area. If you live in London SW1, it is currently £3.50 an hour. It is less in other parts of London and considerably less outside London.

All baby-sitters charge extra for sitting after midnight. If you are in the habit of coming home at 3 am, be prepared to pay for the pleasure. When the children wake you up at 6 am, you may find the pleasure short-lived and not repeat it too often.

Many nanny agencies run baby-sitting services whereby, for a registration fee, usually around £10 per annum, they supply baby-sitters who are local live-in or live-out nannies who want to earn some extra money. Parents have the added assurance of entrusting their offspring to a professional. The charge goes directly to the nanny.

The baby-sitting circle: how it works

A group of parents living within close proximity baby-sit for each other accruing points for the number of evenings they have baby-sat. They keep up an equal number of points, accruing extra points if they sit late at night.

The drawback with this system is that someone has to keep tabs voluntarily on each couple's number of points accrued and do the organising which requires both phoning round and being phoned.

Couples tend to join baby-sitting circles with great enthusiasm and then find the fact that they have to pay back the baby-sitting not very agreeable as it means an evening where one or other of you is out baby-sitting.

Chapter 9

Other Helpers and Services

The cleaning woman

Up and down the country, armies of cleaning women, dailies, chars, Mrs Mops or whatever you care to call them, drag their weary bodies across town for an hourly rate, cash in hand, that the taxman never hears about.

Cleaning women are paid the going rate for the area where they work and there is not a cleaning woman flicking her duster over your mantelpiece who doesn't know exactly what the local going rate is.

In central and north London in 1989 the going rate is £4 per hour with at least two weeks' and usually three weeks' holiday pay, sick pay and all the statutory holidays too. Despite all those benefits, no P45, P46 or P60 forms pass through these ladies' hands, and they are considered casual labour both by their employers and the government. The London area rates are the highest in the country. In many parts of the country holiday and sick pay are also unheard of. In York in 1989 £2.50 is the going rate and an employer would not think of paying anything more than the casual daily rate.

How to find a cleaning woman

Word of mouth has always been the most common way of finding a cleaning woman. You ask a friend if her cleaning woman has a friend and on it goes. This is effective if the cleaning woman is Portuguese, Spanish or Filipino as the women tend to function within each nationality as a large extended family of expatriates, staying close to their fellow nationals, helping each other to find work. There are lots of domestic employment agencies with cleaning women on their books. They expect an agency fee of around two weeks' wages plus VAT, probably with a minimum fee of £30 plus VAT.

The family retainer

Many cleaning women become a fixture of the family and stay with the same family for years, developing a close relationship with everyone and becoming very much part of the family's life. This sort of loyalty has its advantages and its drawbacks. The old faithful cleaner can develop into an emotional burden for her employer who can't bear to sack her, finds it embarrassing to tell her she isn't doing the job properly, and finds her house is not being kept in the state she wants it to be. However, there are fewer and fewer of these treasures around, particularly in the big city where cleaners have a street-wise knowledge of what they should be earning. They also have to keep up with inflation and the cost of living in the city. The solution to having to deal with an individual cleaner is to use a cleaning service.

The cleaning service

In the past ten years cleaning services have started operations all over the country. Little vans with smart names like The Clean Team, Poppies, or Scrubbers disgorge teams of cleaners, clutching their own equipment, who descend on your house and make it gleam in a few hours. There is no emotional commitment to a cleaning service, but the financial commitment is greater.

Look in the Yellow Pages under Cleaning and Maintenance Services and you will find them listed by the dozen.

Poppies is the biggest cleaning service in the UK with agencies all over the country. Its head office is in Darlington in County Durham. The regional agencies charge the going rate for the part of the country they are in. For example, in London the rate is £7 per hour (including VAT) for a general clean, £9 per hour for a spring clean; in Darlington a general clean is £4.50 per hour.

Some cleaning services send an individual cleaner, others always supply cleaners in teams. The Clean Team in north London charges £25 per hour (plus VAT) sending in teams of three who will work for as long as necessary (minimum one hour) doing either a general clean or a spring clean.

The great advantage of a cleaning service is that you employ them when you want them, and they come when you want them. The disaster of the regular daily who has flu on the day of the big party never occurs because an agency has a back-up network of cleaners.

The power struggle

Once you have had a cleaner for a long time, it is difficult to tell her you don't like the way she is doing something. With a cleaning service you can avoid this altogether by having an exact quote for the job which you can constantly refer back to if you don't feel things are being done properly. If you don't like the person the agency sends, they will simply send someone else.

Worries

You don't have to be at home for an agency cleaner any more than you have to be at home for your daily. Most customers leave a set of house keys with the agency who security code them to ensure total protection. Theft is not a problem as the staff of a good agency are in their permanent employ working on a regular basis. Agencies can't carry insurance against theft as such insurance doesn't exist, but they are all insured against breakages and claims would simply go through their insurance broker. Make sure that an agency you engage is fully insured and that they do not use casual labour.

Ironing services

Most cleaning services have an ironing service as well, either charged at the same hourly rate as the cleaning or charged by individual item. Shirts are always charged separately and the charges vary enormously from company to company. Individual ironing services are popping up all over the country. Students often provide ironing services as a way of earning extra money. Look for cards in your local newsagent. Iron Out started up a few years ago in east London. They provide a pick-up and delivery service, charging 60p for a pound of ironing and 35p for a shirt. Business is booming and they hope to expand in parts of London where working parents need their sort of service.

Moving house

Moving house comes close after death and childbirth as one of life's most traumatic experiences. The work of moving house is monumental and if you are holding down a job and running a family, the process can take months out of your life. Day-to-day living among the, as yet, unattacked boxes, searching for a third coffee mug, can be unbearable. Check to see if a local cleaning agency provides a house-moving service. Poppies does for one. Treat yourself well. Pay for the service and minimise the inconvenience.

Domestic services and time savers

Domestic workaholics are made, not born. Most are made by growing up watching a mother wear herself ragged, trying to do the work of ten. Almost all domestic chores can be delegated to a service business that will be more than happy to undertake them. Delegating is a great art. It is a key management skill, greatly prized in business as it is the major lubricant to the smooth running of any enterprise.

The mental hurdle you need to leap over in a single bound is the concept of *paying* for services to make your domestic life easier. Money makes the world go around, and if you want your domestic. world to go round, you have to be willing to part with some in order to put your feet up and relax.

If you have a confectioner make the space-shuttle shaped birthday cake of your child's dreams, when you carry it into the darkened room, candles alight, singing 'Happy Birthday to You', your proud and delighted offspring isn't going to dismiss it because you weren't in the kitchen until 3 am, clutching the cake decorator.

Dinner parties

Remember the dinner party? That was when you invited six or eight friends around, before the children were born of course, to sample the gourmet delights of an inventive day on your part in the kitchen. Who has dinner parties any more? People whose children have grown up, people with loads of money, and people with a reasonable amount of money who like to entertain their friends and who don't have the time to do it themselves and call in a caterer, that's who. Look in the Yellow Pages under Caterers and you will find endless small caterers, many of them women running small businesses, willing to come round and put on a lovely dinner party for you for a reasonable price.

Caterers report that working women don't employ them for the small dinner party, using them only for business entertaining and family events such as weddings or funerals. Women tend to be guilt-ridden about not being able to manage the small dinner party themselves. Instead, they stop giving them and subject their 100 most intimate friends to a yearly 'get rid of last year's social obligations' mob scene where, squeezed into a living room designed to accommodate no more than ten, untrained teenagers shove plates of damp hors d'oeuvres around, slopping wine as they go.

This is unnecessary punishment, both for yourself and for your friends.

It has taken us no time at all to get used to the dramatic changes in, for example, grocery shopping that have only occurred in the last half of the 1980s. In 1989 supermarkets open at 8 am and close at 8 pm. It is only a matter of time until some are open, as has been the case in America for years, around the clock.

Convenience foods abound that are delicious – even to someone over 16. Ready-made, frozen party foods from Marks & Spencer are fresh and delectable.

Masochistic home management by the modern working mother must be made a thing of the past, and you are in the forefront of the movement.

Personal domestic service is becoming big business. Sadly, working mothers are not yet major customers. Managers report that the average British woman is just not used to using that sort of service. Their main customers are male yuppies from the City and wealthy social women, without jobs, both of whom are used to paying to get things done.

How to find personal domestic services

You can't do it by looking in the Yellow Pages. There is no entry under 'Party' for businesses that come in and organise your party. They are listed under Caterers. Businesses that provide a whole range of services from filling your deep-freeze to walking the dog have no wish to be listed in Personal Services between Karina who offers a special massage and Global Escorts, who provide an escort for every requirement. Word of mouth, advertising in glossy magazines and the card popped through your letter box are the major ways of discovering that these businesses exist.

Jenny Watling, an Australian ex-paediatric nurse, set up Personal Services for busy people with hectic lives. Her company will do anything either on a one-off or a regular basis. For a basic rate of between £7.50 and £10 per hour, Personal Services will do the shopping, walk the dog, mind the children, office-sit, plan your party, weed the garden or anything you need done *by someone else* to make your life easier. Jenny says they love a challenge and will try anything.

Personal Services
11 Bolton Gardens, London SW5 0AL; 01-370 4340

Isobel Simpson started Chatelaine Holiday Homecare in 1988 and can't think now why she didn't start up earlier. She will make sure your empty house is visited daily while you are away so that pets are fed, plants are watered, and potential burglars are persuaded the house is occupied. She will prepare the house for your homecoming, stocking the fridge, putting fresh linen on the beds and even spring-clean if required.

Chatelaine Holiday Homecare
17 Durham Terrace, London W2 5PB; 01-221 1465

Fait Accompli, run by Camilla Lawman and Kate Menzies, offers a party planning service, top-to-toe house service, a travel service where they will get tickets, deliver documents and make reservations for you, and a crisis line where they will, for example, wait around for the plumber while you get on with your life.

Fait Accompli
32b Queensgate Mews, London SW7 5QN; 01-581 0384

Organisation Unlimited International will take over any domestic chore. Employing students and people between jobs, they claim they can do anything.

Organisation Unlimited International
117 Sydney Street, London SW3 6NG; 01-351 0295

Nappy services, shopping services, you name it and you will find someone starting a business to do it. If you want to start your own business, keep the idea to yourself until you've got it established.

You will notice that all these businesses are located in the most monied part of London. Proprietors want to be close to their source of customers. As people get used to paying for services, these sorts of businesses will abound, spreading to the suburbs and all over the country.

If you are still exhausted, need help in managing your life and want to get away from it all, the following is for you.

The Hen House is a women's holiday centre in a handsome 16-bedroom Georgian manor house in its own grounds in the beautiful Lincolnshire wolds. It functions as a hotel exclusively for women, but also runs a programme of special events, courses and workshops aimed at helping women to sort out their lives. The 1989 selection covers relationship and personal direction training, workshops and courses, as well as writing and music weekends. For a brochure, write to:

The Hen House
Hawerby Hall, North Thoresby, Lincolnshire DN36 5QL;
0472 840278

Superwoman does not exist. Good managers do. Unload the domestic workload so you can enjoy your family and your friends.

Children's holiday services

Easter and summer holidays
If there is anything worse for children than going to school, it is not going to school, particularly over the long summer break. It's even worse if it rains every day.

The traditional school summer holiday is not long in Britain, usually little over six weeks, starting in the middle of July and lasting until the beginning of September. What to do with school-age children over this period can be a serious problem. Grannie usually welcomes a visit from the grandchildren for a week, at best two. Your own family holiday will take up part of the time. That still leaves three or four weeks unaccounted for. There are cheap solutions, expensive solutions and very expensive solutions.

Play projects in local primary schools and community centres take place over the Easter and summer holiday period, in summer usually for only four weeks. The projects are designed to help the working parent, starting at 9 am and finishing at 5.30 or 6 pm. Whether the play project is organised by a local parent's group or by the local authority, the authority will provide you with a list of projects in your area. Local authorities run projects through the Play Service in the Recreation Department, through the Social Services Department or under the Education Service. Play projects can also be run by parents or parents' associations on a voluntary basis. The parents' association, having started the project, would apply for a grant from the borough. The play leaders are paid by the borough directly or by the project by means of the grant. The charges are always minimal – some ask only for a donation hoping the parents will pay what they can afford. All are dependent on parent donations for extras.

That is the cheap solution. Here is the expensive one.

Children who do not attend the local primary may not be keen to attend a play project. One of the problems created by sending a child away to school is that his friends are cast far and wide about the country and organising companionship during holiday periods can become complicated and time-consuming. Going to the office is a lot less demanding in time, effort and energy than trying to organise activities to keep a child occupied during the holidays.

PGL Adventures was the first to introduce summer camp activity holidays in Britain in the early 1960s. Camp Beaumont opened for business in 1980 offering day camp facilities. PGL and Beaumont are the leaders in this business, both offering residential and day camping activities in Britain as well as holidays abroad. With PGL the emphasis is on residential holidays. Camp Beaumont prides itself on its day camps. There are other companies in the summer camp business and you can find out about all of them by phoning the British Tourist Authority and asking for details of holidays for children and teenagers.

Both PGL and Beaumont offer nursery camps taking children as young as three. The nursery campers, aged three to five, are kept separate from the older campers and attended by qualified nursery nurses or infant teachers.

The costs range from a minimal £60 for a mini-break, around £100 per week for day camp, an average cost for residential holidays of around £200 per week, to the spectacular £1445 for a 12-day escorted trip to Florida to Space Camp and Disney World.

Catherine Wiley, Camp Secretary of Camp Beaumont, regards Camp Beaumont as providing a service for working parents. The main attraction for working parents is the pick-up and delivery service. There are 500 pick-up points all over London, but if you are unable to get your child to a pick-up point and wait with him, the camp monitors (counsellors) operate a door-to-door service. The day camp organisation accepts the fact that parents have their own schedules and allows parents to drop children at camp before it starts, for example at 8.45 where camp proper starts at 9.45. It will allow parents to collect as late as 5.30. Camp itself finishes at 4.45 pm. The children are not left alone and miserable waiting for a parent to arrive but are involved in supervised activities until collected.

PGL and Beaumont offer organised collection by rail, coach and even aeroplane for their residential camps.

Group leaders, counsellors or monitors. By whatever name they are, by and large, teachers, undergraduates and students from teacher training colleges. They are over 18. The ratio of camper to counsellor is 1 to 5, the youngsters are kept in small groups limited to their own age group and the level of supervision is high.

The range of activities offered by the camping companies is spectacular, and, if you can afford it, a terrific way to keep your children entertained during the summer.

Camp Beaumont
9 West Street, Godmanchester, Huntingdon, Cambridgeshire PE18 8HG; 0480 56123

PGL Young Adventure Ltd
Station Street, Ross-on-Wye, Herefordshire HR9 7AH; 0989 768768

Short-term solutions for the odd weekend or week-day childcare are available in the form of small hotels specifically for children. One example of a successful business providing short-term relief is The Little House in Fulham, London.

The Little House
1 Tyrawley Road, London SW6 4QS; 01-731 5805; 01-731 6298

The Little House is a business set up by a mother and her nanny taking in children for short periods, not only during the day but also for overnight stays. They will take in children of any age and provide a day and residential service.

They are inspected annually by the council and run on the specifications of a nursery school. They are offering their clients the extra benefit of an emergency service and an overnight service. The selling feature is that a home from home is offered, a cosy, loving atmosphere that a child can readily adapt to.

Six children may be staying at any one time. When a child is going to stay overnight, he should be brought to them at tea-time. The child then has time for playing, tea, a bath and a story by which time he should be happy and settled in. The parents collect the child at noon the next day. His clothes will have been washed and he will have had lots of play and cuddles. The charge for day's stay is £25. An overnight stay costs £50.

Their clients are either regulars who leave their children for a few days a week or mothers who need a break to shop, keep an appointment or simply have a rest. They also have clients who have nannies and bring their children to The Little House on the nanny's day off.

As an emergency or stop-gap solution, this is a wonderful port for the occasional storm in domestic arrangements.

Birthday parties

Entertaining adults is easy. You know in your heart of hearts, if you don't get it entirely right, they will forgive you. Major occasions for children can fill you with dread, fear and loathing because they won't understand if you don't get it right. And they all know what happened at everyone else's party. So do some of the mothers. A mother once entered my house, son in tow for a birthday party, looked in and screeched, 'What, no entertainer!' I survived and so will you.

Look in the Yellow Pages under Entertainers if you want someone to come to the house and either run the whole party or entertain the children with a puppet show or a clown act for part of the party. Word of mouth from the other mums will tell you who is good and who is not, and you will get the complete low-down on every party your child goes to driving him home. There are lots of books on party games and their rules. I was devoted to one called *Party Games for Young Children* by Jayne Grey, published by Ward Lock. It is now out of print but Ward Lock have replaced it with *Children's Party Games* by Michael Johnstone. There are also lots of books available on how to organise children's parties. Jane Asher, the actress, has produced books on both birthday cakes and costumes.

Not all children like party games – or birthday parties for that matter. You will find out very quickly what your children like, and organise their birthdays accordingly.

Shop for all the accoutrements for the party in one of the specialist party shops or specialist departments in big stores. Specialist shops seem to come and go. Barnum's at Olympia, London and Kensington Carnival in London SW10 are still around. Look in the Business and Services Directory under Party and you will find a few listings. Sadly, there aren't enough of them to merit a listing in the Yellow Pages. There is still a great need for the specialist shop that saves the busy mother from having to drag round from store to store buying the favours in one place, buying the balloons and having them printed in another, the cake moulds in another and on and on.

Hold the party at the weekend. Don't expect to drag yourself home from your place of work and have the energy left over to host an event for energetic four-year-olds. Birthday parties need an adult management team of two, if not three adults. Your husband must be there and anyone else you can rope in. Besides, the birthday party after school where the children, clutching their presents and full of anticipation, are collected by the mum in charge, is often a hurtful spectacle for the children who weren't invited.

You can't invite everyone to a birthday party. Keep the numbers small for your own sanity. After each game, little children tend to look at you like the Midwich Cuckoos, waiting for what comes next. They can't entertain themselves like adults do while you are out of the room getting the hors d'oeuvres. The key to a successful birthday party is to have a small and manageable group of children and every second of the party organised.

Presents

Children, from a very young age, know exactly what they want. They also change their minds constantly. As soon as your child is old enough for birthday (and Christmas) presents, make lists based on what your child tells you he wants. When he is old enough to write, get him to make the lists. I say lists, because he won't make just one list. He will make a new list every other day, if not every day. Close to the event, check that you have got in your possession the last definitive list and go out and buy within reason and what you can afford from the list. You can either give children what you think they want, or what you think they should think they want, or what they really want. My own experience has taught me that if you want to have a truly happy child who is over the moon because he has had the *best birthday ever*, get him what he's asked for and leave the improving toys to Aunt Maud.

Chapter 10

Schools

Primary school

You must by law send your child to school in the term following his fifth birthday. Most schools accept children in the infant school at what is called 'rising five', meaning the school year in which the child will turn five. Schools vary greatly as to when they will accept children. The Education Office of your local borough will be able to tell you at what stage of 'rising five' they admit children to school. You can put your child's name on the list of a county school no earlier than one year before eventual admission.

Primary schools can be private, county or voluntary. A county school has to take your child if you live within its catchment area. Private schools have some sort of entry examination or interview and make their own choice. Voluntary schools have a religious foundation and entry is determined by governing bodies. The governors of voluntary schools are responsible for admissions policy, accept children who conform to the admissions policy and don't have to accept children who do not. Voluntary schools at present are Church of England, Catholic and Jewish. The resources and funding available to them provided by the local authority is identical to the funding of the county schools.

When you are deciding where to send your child to school a number of decisions have to be made and many questions answered. You have a choice of private or state education, and in state education, voluntary or council.

Points to consider

- At what age are you going to send your child to school: rising five or five plus?
- What is the choice near your home? What sort of travelling time is involved in driving or walking the child to school? Where will the new friends be if the school is a good distance from home?

- Is there an active parents' association and will you be expected to participate?
- Are parents expected to help in the classroom?
- Are parents expected to help with their child's reading and arithmetic at home?
- How many are there in a class? How are the classes organised? What system is there to keep you informed about your child's progress and confidence?
- What provision is there for your child's special needs, be they learning difficulties or physical disabilities?
- What provision is there for your children after school when you are working full time?

After school and holidays

For working parents, after school and holiday time can present a real problem. The only answer is to get involved. You can do this both by developing your own network of friends and by joining established national and local organisations.

National Out of School Alliance (NOOSA)
Oxford House, Derbyshire Street, Bethnal Green Road, London E2 6HG; 01-739 4787

This registered charity offers practical advice in the form of research, funding applications, legal responsibility, conferences where local need is identified and general information about how to find an out of school scheme in your area, and how to start one if none exists. It publishes *Starting from Scratch, Legal Responsibility and Finding the Money* as well as *Out of School in London*.

There is great variety in what the after-school clubs have to offer, their size and the cost. Some are held in play-centres, community centres or council facilities, while others take place in people's homes. The children are collected from school and usually go to the scheme on foot where they are given a snack and kept there until their parents collect them at approximately 6 pm. The cost relates to the means of collection, on foot or by minibus, how substantial the snack is and how much they are subsidised by the local borough.

Private schools

Who sends their children to fee-paying schools? Almost everyone who can afford to, it seems. Two-income families now facilitate entry for children, whose ancestors could not have dreamt of a such thing, into the hallowed halls of privileged and private education. Fifty-seven per cent of students in fee-paying education are what the Headmaster's Conference terms 'first-time buyers'. Gone are the sons of the vicars and school-teachers whose salaries can no longer begin to provide private education for their children. They have been replaced by a flood of parents with the means, often provided by a second income, to secure what they believe to be a better quality of education for their children.

The number of children in the independent sector continues to rise despite the fact that the fees also continue to rise and well above the rate of inflation. The Independent Schools Information Service (ISIS) found that in 1988, while the number of school-aged children dropped by 2 per cent, pupil numbers at fee-paying schools increased by 1.7 per cent.

Apparently, children can't start early enough. In 1988 the number of pupils between the ages of two and eight rose by 4.8 per cent in preparatory schools.

This increase has occurred despite the mounting costs that can be as high as £1800 a term for a full boarder, and this is out of taxed income, the parents having already contributed to the rejected state system of education through rates and taxes.

Professional parents want to be more involved in their children's education and the schools are competing in the market-place. Any school, particularly one dependent on boarding, listens to the needs of the parents. Sensible schools run coaches to bring children into town for the weekend, at least three weekends a term. Weekly boarding is becoming more common.

Eton, according to the headmaster of Haileybury, David Jewell, is the only really national school left in Britain with an intake from all over the country. The rest are finding that parents are attracted to a school if it is within reasonable reach of home. Parents and parent interest have become part of the landscape. The headmaster who defines the parent as 'a nuisance created by the motor car'[1] is no longer in touch with his students or his parents.

Weekly boarding, which allows students a relaxed family life at the weekend with the discipline of school during the weekday is on the increase. The number of pupils boarding only on weekday nights rose in 1988 by 9.4 per cent, the greatest increase in weekly

1. From *The Chance of a Lifetime: A Study of Boarding Education*, R. Lambert, Weidenfeld & Nicolson, 1975. Quoted in *Private Schools and Public Issues*, Irene Fox, Macmillan.

boarding being in London and the south east. From September 1989 Highgate School, in north London, will cease its full boarding, converting to weekly boarding only. Highgate has also dropped Saturday morning school, responding to the work patterns of the parents whose mothers want their sons home on Saturday. Highgate considers itself a local school with a specific catchment area of local boys, the majority of whom have professional parents.

There are arguments for and against weekly boarding; some schools feel it turns the children without family or parents close by, and particularly children whose parents are abroad, into second-class citizens. Haileybury, for example, has lots of boys from overseas and one of its strengths, greatly valued by the parents who live abroad, is organised events over the weekends.

A boarding school has a much more formative influence over a child because the child is there for so much more of his time. A child is only at a day school for a limited period, and the school is bound to have a limited influence.

All boarding schools allow children home for a certain number of weekends. At prep schools the children generally remain in school for five weekends a term. The schools feel strongly that this helps to socialise the children and teaches them a lot about being together. The weekends in school also allow the parents to go away for the weekend. The weekends with the children are then greatly looked forward to by both parents and children.

As they get older, boarders are allowed greater freedom, depending on the school. In general less freedom is still given to the girls than the boys. In the sixth form most students are allowed to go out on Sundays.

None of the heads I interviewed said they could identify which children had working mothers or not. They commented that they might be able to identify by a child's behaviour and attitude whether he had a good mother or a bad mother, but not whether he had a working mother. Guilt about having sent the child away to school, particularly if this is not a family tradition, results in the parent being, if anything, considerably more involved and conscientious.

Are parents giving their children a wonderful opportunity or banishing them so they can get on with their own lives? The answer to this depends entirely on who you speak to and your own feelings.

Obviously, public boarding school heads feel that children benefit from boarding. At a boarding school, all the activities happen under one roof and the child isn't being driven from pillar to post for a variety of activities, most of which he hates anyway. Being a child can be hard work for those whose parents have great expectations.

Having to be good and clever and talented can be exhausting. The boarding school gives the child the chance to be himself, to stand and stare. A number of boarding heads commented that parents delude themselves that they are having a family life, keeping the children at home, when they aren't. When a boarding school child comes home for a weekend, the stress has gone, nagging is unnecessary and parents can simply enjoy their children. The children look forward to coming home and the parents look forward to having them home. A boarding school provides a child with an objective environment wherein he can lead his own life, have his privacy and actually have a childhood. The rush of busy parents and city life often deprives a child of this.

The discipline can do wonders in adverse conditions. It is said that the cream of Britain's best public schools adjusted much more easily and readily to the rigours of life in Japanese prisoner of war camps in the Far East during the last war than the men who had got far too used to freedom, comfort and affection in their East End childhoods.

Parents are supposed to want their children to be happy. All children are different. Some children love boarding school, some are neutral, a few loathe it. Some parents believe they are investing in deferred happiness, the long-term benefits of a boarding education being more important than immediate happiness. Mothers tend to be more concerned about their children's happiness which inspired a father to remark, 'They go to public school for a number of reasons, one of which is not to be blissfully happy.'[2] This is a traditional attitude which may be anathema to you. There is still a lot of traditional thinking among the heads of boarding schools. One reminded me that most British people don't really like young children anyway.

Statistics show that the number of students boarding for the full school year fell with the day pupils continuing an upward increase of 2.4 per cent in 1988 compared with the previous year. This might be an indication that the British do, in fact, like their children and want not only to be the most profound influence on their development as opposed to the school, but also to have them around.

Co-educational or single sex

Single sex schools are exempt under the Sex Discrimination Act but not under the Equal Opportunities Act. Any school taking girls at the age of 13 would lose their exemption. Many schools take the

2. *Private Schools and Public Issues – The Parent's View*, Irene Fox, Macmillan, 1985.

decision that they don't want to become bogged down in this. Boys and girls are very different as teenagers, developing and maturing at very marked and different rates. There are many excellent girls' schools and heads of boys' schools are loath to poach the talent from them. They would also have to face the dilemma of either halving the number of boys or doubling the size of the school if they were to admit girls.

However, financial need and a wish to maintain or even raise the academic standard has prompted some traditional boarding schools to go co-educational, Marlborough being an example. Heads tend to have strong views on this move. Marlborough, it is felt, is being totally honest in that it is becoming co-educational throughout the school. Boys' schools which accept girls in the sixth form only are looking at their academic standards and not at a changed philosophy of education. Girls who join a school in the sixth form are the high-flyers, *la crème de la crème*. In the end they can badly upset the balance, leaving the boys feeling more than somewhat inadequate. This is hardly going to promote a more accepting and relaxed attitude on the part of the boys in their developing relationships with girls. The girls themselves are often lonely and isolated, missing the comradeship of their girls' schools.

Boys resent the tarting up of formerly spartan surroundings to be fit for use by the girls. Central heating in bathrooms and other sybaritic excesses suddenly start to appear. However, parents generally no longer expect either male or female children to sleep on hair mattresses in ice cold rooms. But children who have been to a co-educational boarding prep often find single sex education disagreeable, and want to go on to co-educational boarding schools such as Bedales or Bryanston.

Cost

Educating your children privately is not cheap. There are a number of saving and pension schemes. It is best to obtain expert guidance for the long-term commitment of paying school fees. Go to the experts for advice.

Where to get educational advice

The two leaders in the field of advice-giving for private education are Gabbitas, Truman & Thring and ISIS. They function quite differently.

What you should expect to pay

Average fees per term (1989–90)

Area	Boarding fee	Weekly boarding fee	Day fee Boarding school	Day fee Day school
	£	£	£	£
Scotland	2039	2060	1119	791
Wales	1779	—	1194	—
Ireland	1430	1308	722	609
England:				
North	1955	1577	1163	778
W Midlands	2208	2172	1454	842
E Midlands	2085	1665	1292	1018
E Anglia	2001	1849	1287	1050
South West	2084	1873	1278	873
Gtr London	2309	2486	1444	1055
South East	2196	1877	1511	929
Average	2086	1835	1319	874

Table supplied by ISIS, April 1989

These are only the fees. There is always a considerable outlay at the beginning on the uniform and sports equipment which have to be replenished constantly. At the day schools, school meals have to be paid for as well as optional membership of the Old Boys Society.

Gabbitas, Truman & Thring
Broughton House, 6–8 Sackville Street, Piccadilly, London W1X 2BR; 01-734 0161 or 01-439 2071

Gabbitas, Truman & Thring is a non-profit making charitable trust. If you get in touch, you will be sent a range of well-produced brochures describing various services, without charge.

They offer advice to parents about suitable schools free of charge, often over the phone, as well as a counselling service which is of particular use to parents from abroad, first-time buyers or children with special educational needs, providing advice from nursery school to tertiary education. They offer a comprehensive guardianship service to parents who are abroad. They publish *Which School*, a guide to independent education for children from 5–18 as well as specialised guides to independent Further Education, Boarding schools and colleges, and English language schools.

As a non-profit making trust, any surplus income is devoted to bursaries for children in need. The bursaries are of two kinds. Long-term bursaries are available to anyone who is in real difficulty over payment of school fees. Priority is given to the children of Anglican clergy and teachers and is based on need with the provision that the child involved maintains a good standard of work, receiving good reports, and that the financial need of the parents remains the same. Short-term emergency bursaries are also granted, usually to assist a pupil to complete an examination course where a major family financial problem has arisen. In this case the school's endorsement of the application would be expected.

The role of Gabbitas is to find the best place and the best solution for the student. The extent of the advice their service can provide ranges from pre-preparatory education to counselling on selecting the right university or college or even career.

GTT will even give people advice before they have started a family as to what is available. After the child is born, the advice is based on the best interests of the child.

While they can offer advice on public boarding schools all over the country, they can only give factual advice on day schools outside London. In London they can provide inside information on all the day schools. They also offer advice on programmes during the school holidays, courses and summer camps.

If you come to GTT with an immediate problem of placing your child, they will advise you regarding a suitable school that has a vacancy. They will not advise you to try and get your child into a school that is full. However, schools are not terribly efficient about informing GTT about vacancies so you may be lucky applying at short notice to a school without a vacancy if you are trying to get an older, academically able child in. If, on the other hand, you are seeking counselling well in advance to applying to any school, GTT will inform you of all the possibilities, and how and when to apply. Parents are often not aware of the vast variety of schools available. GTT is accustomed to advising the first-time buyer.

They now offer a wide-ranging counselling service where an experienced consultant, in an in-depth interview with parents (and child if appropriate), offers expert guidance through the maze of the British educational system. The charge is £80 plus VAT. Additional fees are charged up to £125 for advice regarding guardianship, university or polytechnic entrance, making special arrangements for a client and assessment by an educational psychologist.

Gabbitas, Truman & Thring will not give advice in areas where

143

they are not expert. They will direct parents to an agency that can help them (for example, advice regarding a handicapped child). In other words, the advice is all-encompassing and, where they cannot supply it, they will direct the parents to the people who can.

Advice is not confined to children in the fee-paying sector. They will, for example, advise a 16-year-old who wants to transfer out of the state system into the fee-paying sector for A levels.

Who pays Gabbitas?

They have just instituted the fee for the specialised counselling services. Hitherto all their income, and still the vast proportion of it, came from commissions from the schools in which they have placed a child.

Independent Schools Information Service (ISIS)
London and South East Region, 3 Vandon Street, London SW1H 0AN; 01-222 7274

The service ISIS offers is fundamentally different from that offered by Gabbitas. It is not their function to recommend individual schools, but rather to list schools so that parents can make their own choice. Gabbitas, on the other hand, recommends students to a suitable school with a vacancy at the time the student is seeking a place.

They are not only a national but also an international network of bureaux, giving people advice on everything from nursery schools, kindergartens, placement and counselling. They advise from infancy through public school and will advise at a higher, tertiary level what to study but not where. They also advise on summer programmes.

ISIS publishes leaflets covering the whole gamut of planning and information necessary to a parent before deciding how to proceed. These extremely practical leaflets cover diverse matters from 'Questions to ask when you visit a school' to 'How grandparents can help with schools fees'.

ISIS has both national and international offices and matches up foreign students to the British system as well as advising on private education in the USA, Canada and the EC. It publishes a handbook, *What is ISIS?* and also a quarterly newspaper. In the handbook it lists insurance brokers and insurance companies who are able to give advice on school fees emphasising that this cannot be embarked on too early.

Their counselling costs are less than Gabbitas at £40 per hour.

Who pays ISIS?

Schools submit information to ISIS and must be accredited. They pay ISIS a certain amount per year per number of students and are listed in a handbook.

The new handbook indicates more clearly which schools do weekly boarding. This is in response to the demand that children come home for the weekend.

ISIS will send you on request a comprehensive book on schools in London and South-East England which includes a map with a key for every school, girls' and boys', junior and senior, co-educational and specialist. It costs £1.50 (including p & p).

Information and handbooks about independent schools in other regions may be obtained, enclosing two first-class stamps, from:

ISIS Headquarters
56 Buckingham Gate, London SW1E 6AG; 01-630 8790

There are a number of books available listing schools and offering either straight factual information or inside information about the atmosphere of the school.

The Good School Guide: Amanda Atha and Sarah Drummond (Harpers and Queen)
Contains information about 250 schools which is not only factual but also more personal. It tells you what the students are like and describes the atmosphere.

Public and Preparatory Schools Yearbook (annual) edited by J F Burnet, (A & C Black)
Separate editions for boys and girls. Gives a history of each school, a list of the members of staff and their qualifications and tells you everything you need to know about admission requirements, religious education, curriculum, games and scholarships. The information is factual.

The Schools Book: edited by Klaus Boehm and Jenny Lees-Spalding (Papermac)
Contains facts about 550 schools but doesn't describe the atmosphere of the school.

Chapter 11

Sick Children

'Mummy, I don't feel well!'

For the working mother, these are the most feared words in the English language. Small children are liable to sudden high temperatures, stomach aches, short-lived flus and colds that come on, usually in the night without warning, and almost always when the next day at the office is the most important day of your life.

'It couldn't have happened at a worse time' is the oft-heard description of the timing of a child's illness. In fact, if you examine your life, every day could not be a worse day for your child to be ill. A sick child who needs to be cared for at home stops you from fulfilling the particular responsibilities of any particular day.

How you feel about suddenly having to postpone or cancel meetings or simply miss a day's work depends very much on your own personality, how conscientious you are both regarding your job and regarding your child. Take your pick.

If you have a nanny, a mother's help or an au pair, your problems are easily solved because there is someone with a meaningful relationship to your child in the house. If you have a reliable daily who has a relationship with the children, she might also be used as a stop-gap.

Nursery schools will not accept a child who is poorly and it is unfair to try to leave your child in school when he is blowing and sneezing and liable to infect the other children. If your child becomes ill in the middle of the day, the school will call you and expect you to collect him. They will not take kindly to your prevaricating, asking the school to hold on for a few more hours. They expect someone to come as soon as possible to collect an unwell child both for the child's sake and for the sake of the other children.

A minder will not accept an unwell child for the same reasons and will also call the responsible parent if there is any sign that the child is unwell.

What do you do?

If you have family close by, the family will usually take over if the situation is desperate. A large percentage of working mothers in Britain leave their children with family anyway. What about the rest of the mothers?

First, here is one of the most important crises where the development of your own extended family of friends is crucial. The Working Mothers Association with its 70 branches up and down the country was set up to function in exactly that way, as a large extended family of working mothers prepared to help each other out. However, with a sick child who is also infectious, you are not going to find it easy to get someone to come round and sit with your child, particularly if it involves bringing her own children with her.

Have a close relationship with an agency which you know can provide you with help at a moment's notice. Karen Southam who set up The Nicest Nannies in north London a few years ago runs an emergency service to cover just such crises as the suddenly ill child for the mother who, for example, must be in court the following morning. She has dependable floating nursery nurses and experienced women who will come at a moment's notice.

What is it going to cost?

A lot! This is an area where the most terrible stress is produced because mothers want to find a solution to a sudden crisis without having to pay through the nose. If you don't have a close family who can come at a moment's notice, you simply have to swallow hard and pay the going rate. Costs will vary slightly up and down the country but in general you will pay an agency fee of approximately £20 for finding someone for the day. It is much more sensible to book the emergency carer for a week and pay a weekly rate which would probably be about £40. The nursery nurse herself will charge between £3.00 and £3.50 an hour. You will find yourself paying the weekly rate for a nursery nurse of anything between £120 and £180.

If your child is seriously ill at home and you cannot afford to pay a carer to come in and stay with him, and if you have no family close by to help you out in the long term, you and your husband will have to make arrangements with your employers for compassionate leave, leave for parental reasons, holiday leave or unpaid leave.

As medicine has improved, fewer children need to go into hospital and those who do, stay for less time than was necessary a decade ago. However, more parents both go out to work and do not have the resources to take care of a child convalescing at home.

This creates a new problem for families with a sick child, and particularly for families with a chronically ill child. Where the NHS is able to save money with shorter stays in hospital and out-patient treatment, the financial burden now falls on the family. The need for paid leave to care for or to share in the care of a sick child is becoming an important issue.

A child whose parents have arranged reliable live-out or outside childcare has got to be found alternative arrangements when he is ill. The psychological effect of illness and hospital treatment in the company of strangers can leave lasting scars on a child. Sometimes parents are left with no alternative but to indulge in deception, taking, at worst, personal sick leave, unpaid leave or annual holiday leave. Some local government bodies have made some provision, mainly councils such as Camden or Haringey. Camden allows 25 days per year. Businesses and employers may be considerably more sympathetic and flexible than the employee realises. All the mothers I spoke to were either in full-time or part-time employment and reported that, despite the lack of any kind of legislation for 'leave for parental reasons', their and their husband's employers were sympathetic to the crisis and allowed them time off. One mother, employed part time by Boots, reported that Boots were both sympathetic and attuned to the needs of female married staff. She was totally confident that her employer understood her predicament and would let her stay with her child for as long as necessary. She would be allowed leave of absence after her holidays ran out which would cause financial hardship, but this could not be helped.

All the mothers said that anyone taking advantage of a company and exploiting their compassionate leave would be immediately spotted. Genuine family problems were easily identified and no one could get away with taking advantage of a sympathetic employer.

The National Association for the Welfare of Children in Hospital (see page 149) issues publications but cannot do more to help the parent of an ill child than give information about current government policy regarding staying with a child either at home or in hospital.

Admitting your child to hospital

If your child arrives at the hospital because of an emergency or an accident, he may be placed in an adult ward, depending on the nature of his illness and the wishes of the consultant. However, if the admission is elective, your child should be placed in a paediatric ward and parents should, if possible, ensure that their child is going to a hospital where there is a children's ward. If none is available, the matter is out of the parents' hands. Where there is a choice, the best place for a child is with other children under the supervision of staff who are trained to deal with infants and children.

Separate provision for teenagers is rare. Most teenagers are still put in adult wards which can be emotionally trying for both them and the adults around them.

Staying with your child

The National Association for the Welfare of Children in Hospital (NAWCH) was set up to lobby for the rights of parents to be with their children in hospital.

National Association for the Welfare of Children in Hospital (NAWCH)
Argyle House, 29–31 Euston Road, London NW1 2SD; 01-833 2041

More and more hospitals are willing to allow a parent to stay in the hospital, and hospitals now try to keep children in for shorter periods which makes the disruption easier for the parent. The most important concern for a child who is ill is to have someone on call, not necessarily the mother but someone important to the child. A good paediatric ward is happy to have a relative or even the nanny stay with the child on the basis that the person is well known to the child and providing comfort. Not being able to console the intense grief of a crying child left alone on a ward is an appalling burden for ward staff. For student nurses, it is particularly difficult. A z-bed is usually provided and placed next to the child's bed. The bed is comfortable enough, but tending to a restless, uncomfortable child and the general noise of the hospital leaves the mother very tired.

Mothers have said that they sometimes feel as though their relationship with the child has been put in a gold-fish bowl, being constantly observed by the hospital staff. Mothers worry whether they are being loving enough or responding to their child's needs properly. The nurses are aware and understanding of this anxiety which is, in fact, quite normal. Only a most unconscientious mother wouldn't feel that.

Parents often feel pressurised to stay with a child when they feel they cannot. An enlightened paediatric ward, while aware that people have careers and great demands on their lives, will do everything in their power to convince parents that their child needs them in hospital.

The operation

It has been government policy since 1959 (Platt Report) that parents may be present with a child while he is still conscious before an operation and may be present when he comes round. Insist on it. It is your and your child's right.

What if you cannot stay in hospital?

Working parents, if they are unable to stay during the day, can visit at night and put the child to bed with a story and a cuddle. Make sure the child and staff know when next you are coming. Visiting is especially important during the first few days in hospital, and particularly before and after an operation.

Children can get terribly worked up if they have no idea when you are going to visit them. If necessary, pin a notice on to the bed so that everyone knows when you will be there next. It is often terribly draining for the parents as well because the emotional impact on the child of being in hospital and all that that entails might make the child cry terribly when his parents first appear (perhaps as a sign of relief that they have finally come) or ignore them totally (to punish them for not having come more often).

What if the hospital doesn't want you to stay?

It is government policy that parents should have free access to their children in hospital. If you are denied this, ask to speak to the ward sister. If she is unsupportive, ask to speak to the unit manager. If you find you are meeting resistance, call NAWCH (01-883 2041) for advice and support and inform your local Community Health Council of your experience. Your local GP and health visitor may be able to help, too.

In an old-fashioned and unenlightened children's ward, the attitude of the staff is more often than not the problem, not stated in so many words but conveyed by attitude. The parents seem to get in the way; surely it would be easier for everyone if the child got over his misery and the parents were banished so the staff could get on with their job. Children don't get over it and a familiar caring person is necessary to the child in hospital.

What about other children at home?

If you are a working parent you will already have some sort of care but if you need extra help you could ask your local Social Services Department what they have to offer. The social worker at the hospital will help with this. Some departments will even go so far as to arrange home helps or family care workers who can live in.

Helpful information

NAWCH issues an excellent booklet entitled *Your Child in Hospital: A Parent's Handbook* which informs, advises and answers questions about children in hospital. It lists a number of books for young and older children to help them to cope with being in hospital. (There is also a further reading list for parents.) It is advisable to get this book and read through it before the need occurs as most children are admitted to hospital suddenly and without warning.

The Consumers' Association, publishers of *Which?*, in association with NAWCH produce a small handbook called *Children in Hospital: An Action Guide for Parents*. It is full of information to help parents to cope with their child in hospital from what to pack to who's who in the hospital. The book describes how to prepare the child for the hospital stay and the treatment. Children will eventually adjust to being in hospital. However, it is a process that involves working through three stages of adjustment. Crying and misery give way to a form of mourning which eventually becomes acceptance and adjustment. The long-stay child will have trouble adjusting to being at home again.

Chronic illness

The mothers of children with chronic illnesses whom I interviewed had, of necessity, all taken jobs to accommodate the demands on their time. They gave up their holiday time taking care of their children. One mother worked from 10 pm to 8.30 am in a geriatric home, having given up a day job, so that she could always be available to her child during the day. The girl is a fighter and despite serious problems with kidney failure insists on going to school. Her mother often has to come and fetch her home. This mother reported that financially it is more rewarding to work nights but physically it is too draining to keep up for long. A year and a half of sleeping during the day is as much as she can cope with.

At a higher powered level this becomes more difficult. A mother in advertising said her company was compassionate and trusting but she is not sure what the company's attitude will be if her asthmatic child requires a lot of extra care. Her company, like many new businesses, has a helpful and discretionary attitude to staff with children working a shorter week. However, she didn't think the company itself could stand the strain of her often and prolonged absences because of her child's asthma. She also doubted that *she* could stand the strain of worrying. She felt that eventually the worry would stop her from doing her job properly and that she might ultimately have to consider a long career break.

It helps to have a large family

In general, the mothers found that relatives rallied round, even if they lived a good distance from home. The erosion of the extended family in Britain denies people the sorts of resources, either material or in the form of skills, that people used to rely on. All the mothers I spoke to from ethnic minorities, be they Greek, Hindu, Muslim, Jewish, Italian or other relied on their extended families both financially and in care-giving. If there are no relatives at all to help with the other children in a family, apply to the Social Services Department. In Camden the social services either provided a carer, paid for a carer or provided fostering.

Networking with other mothers in hospital

Whatever problem the mothers faced, they found someone else on the ward who had dealt with it before and found a solution. Networking in the hospital was reported as being very useful in solving domestic problems and in deciding about forms of treatment. In the dialysis unit, the mothers attend a two-week course in the hospital to learn how to manage the dialysis procedure at home. If they are lucky, eventually their children will have a transplant. All these women had no choice but to take the time off and all reported sympathetic employers.

Chapter 12

Children with Special Needs

Children with special needs are children with all forms of disadvantages and disabilities. One child in every 20 is born with some sort of abnormality or defect. Many of these are minor, unimportant and do not impede the child's growth and development. Others require special help. Those children are described as having special needs. The term has come into use as a kind of umbrella description for all children who do not fit easily into the mainstream of life. It isn't always obvious at first that the child has special needs. Conditions as severe as cerebral palsy (spastic) often cannot be diagnosed until the child is at least six months old. Furthermore, the different forms of special need all create their own special difficulties of coping and management for the family. A special need might be caused by a physical, mental or emotional disability.

Whatever the problem, there is a charity, a voluntary organisation, a self-help group or some means through which parents can find help, advice, comfort and reassurance. Whatever road you must tread, someone else has trod it before you and can offer their experience to make your way easier. However, life with a disabled child, and particularly a child who is both physically and mentally disabled, is a serious burden on every member of the family, and all members need help in coping.

Working mothers of children with special needs say that, for them, it isn't a matter of finding time to do a job, but needing to do a job in order to stay sane and keep a perspective on life. A full-time job, unless one has full-time specialist help, is next to impossible to keep up. A part-time job, or a job with generous holidays such as teaching, is an essential outlet.

Finding provision and help is an endless struggle, and often more difficult for parents who appear to be coping well and have the means to support their child. Parents reported their local NHS doctors too overstretched themselves to see the potential in handicapped children, understand their parents' aspirations for them, and therefore take the time to investigate or promote other resources.

One mother reported that her severely physically disabled daughter had had so many infections that in the space of 23 months she had been through 17 courses of antibiotics prescribed by her local doctor. The girl is also hyperactive. After contacting the Hyperactive Children's Group, and changing the girl's diet, not only did the infections diminish but also some of the symptoms of hyperactivity.

Resources tend to go to families who are not able to cope either financially or emotionally. Families who give the impression of coping are, in reality, often living on the edge, and must learn to ask for their share of resources. The presence of a seriously disabled child in a family can badly affect the behaviour of other siblings. There is help available in the form of family counselling and therapy through the local authority and the NHS. Families with a child with special needs need all the help they can get and should not be reluctant to ask.

Conveying the impression that everything is under control is often counter-productive in obtaining the sort of assistance and services needed. Parents who have struggled on, bogged down but surviving the day-to-day slog, have often found that help is only offered after they have come to the end of their tether and broken down.

Private forms of help are expensive, whether in the form of assessment, treatment or private help at home. Fight for as much as you can through the NHS and your local education authority.

The 1944 Education Act required local education authorities to provide education for 'handicapped' children, but the idea that these children should be integrated with other children in ordinary schools only came into being through the Education Acts of 1980 and 1981.

The 1981 Education Act changed the law on educational provision for what were then called handicapped children. Children are no longer stigmatised as physically or mentally handicapped but rather as children with special needs who therefore require *special educational needs*. A great attempt is made now to integrate these children, wherever possible and with the agreement of the parents, into ordinary schools (as stipulated in the Act). The local education authority *must* make an assessment of the child's (over the age of two) special needs and *has a duty* to make special provision for all children from the age of 2 to 16, and to 19 if the child is a registered pupil. The provision offered will be at a school suitable for your child's needs, day or boarding, not necessarily in your area.

If parents wish for an assessment of their child under the age of two the local education authority *must* provide one. The content of the LEA assessment is available to the parents as well as being open to parental contribution. Parents may appeal if they do not agree with the special education provision decided upon. Your local health visitor and social worker will give you information about local services, nurseries, suitable playgroups and assessment centres. The Act says that health authorities have a duty to inform parents if they think that the child has or is likely to have special educational needs.

The list of voluntary societies is endless. One place to find a list of them is in an excellent booklet, *Help Starts Here,* published by:

The Voluntary Council for Handicapped Children
National Children's Bureau, 8 Wakley Street, London EC1V 7QE; 01-278 9441

The booklet covers every aspect of concern from the moment the child is born to advice on further education for children with special educational needs (SEN). It is essential for a family with a child with special needs as it describes all your statutory rights, what financial help you are entitled to and how to get it, how to get special equipment, pre-school, education and further education needs, who to talk to and how to find help.

Contact a Family started as a local group in the London Borough of Wandsworth in 1974 with the aim of encouraging self-help among isolated families. It has been a registered charity since 1979. Ten years on, it is now in touch with over 600 support groups all over the country for parents whose children have special needs. It has acquired considerable expertise in promoting self-help locally and has expanded to enable around 30,000 families and 600 self-help and mutual support groups to be linked to each other.

Contact a Family works with two types of groups: local groups whose children might have any kind of disability and others offering nation-wide support to families where the child has a rare syndrome. Contact is not suitable in all cases, nor does it work out, and parents must want to be available to other families with similar problems to participate.

Families with children with severe physical disabilities often find themselves ostracised by their own relatives who, failing to recognise the hurt involved, seldom invite the family with the child. Strangers are kind but don't want to become involved. Being put in touch with other families who have also experienced the sense of isolation, helplessness, and even anger, is of enormous value.

Contact a Family
16 Strutton Ground, London SW1P 2HP; 01-222 2695/3639

Financial help

The Department of Social Security issues a booklet, *A Guide to Non-contributory Benefits for Disabled People* (DSS Booklet HB5). It is essential to have this, as it guides you through the labyrinth of financial help that you are entitled to.

You can obtain DSS booklets or leaflets from your local social security office, your social worker or by post from DSS Leaflets, PO Box 21, Stanmore, Middlesex HA7 1AY.

Care of a handicapped child is expensive and demanding and not something that one person can take on single-handed. This has been recognised and the state has a number of provisions that lighten the load and lessen the burden.

Attendance allowance, DSS Leaflet NI 205. This is tax free and not related to your family income and covers day or night care, £22, and day and night care, £32.95 (1989 rates). It cannot be paid for a child under two, but there is no upper age limit. It applies to anyone who needs a lot of looking after by another person because of mental or physical disability.

Family Credit. If you are a lone parent, or have need of supplementary income, you can apply for Family Credit. Family Credit replaced FIS, Family Income Supplement, in April 1989. It is a regular weekly tax-free non-contributory payment to working people who are responsible for at least one child under the age of 16 (or 19 if in full-time education). You don't need to have paid NICs (National Insurance contributions) to qualify. Family Credit is an *income-related* benefit whereby the amount you receive depends on your or your partner's earnings and savings. Your social security office will be able to tell you about it. Ask for DSS booklet NI 261 *A Guide to Family Credit*.

Aids for the Disabled, DSS Leaflet HB2. You are not expected to finance adaptations to your house to accommodate your child's disability entirely out of your own pocket. Apply to your local authority Social Services Department for help and advice on adaptations to your home and consult the leaflet.

Invalid Care Allowance, DSS Leaflet NI 212. This is taxed but not means-tested and it is for those who must stay at home to care for a handicapped person. You qualify for ICA if you are male or female, married or single, looking after someone who is getting the Attendance Allowance or Constant Attendance Allowance. The rate is £26.20, plus an extra £8.95 for each dependent child and £15.65 for a dependent adult (1989 rates).

Mobility, DSS leaflet NI 211. If your child is unable to walk, he qualifies for this allowance after the age of five. It is a tax-free weekly cash benefit unrelated to any other benefit you might be getting and is a flat rate of £23.05 (1989 rates).

Child Benefit. Every family receives child benefit of £7.25 per week (1989 rate). On top of this you may also qualify for support from Family Credit.

Special care and special nannies

There are many nannies who have done their NNEB training or trained nurses who have a special interest in working with children with handicaps. You can contact any college offering the NNEB course and enquire if there are any girls with a special interest in working with the handicapped, or you can advertise in:

Nursing Times
4 Little Essex Street, London WC2R 3LF; Classified ads: 01-836 6633

The Lady
Classified Advertising Department, 39–40 Bedford Street, London WC2E 9ER (no ads by phone)

Nursery World
Childcare Classified Department, Nursery World Ltd, The Schoolhouse Workshop, 51 Calthorpe Street, London WC1X 0HH; 01-837 7224

Be honest and direct about your child's special need and, if you are lucky, you will find an appropriate and committed girl.

Nannies whose charges have special needs not only need extra dedication but also extra support and sympathy. There is a group called the Special Care Nanny Group, set up by the Special Care Agency to give nannies working for families with handicapped children the back-up, sympathy and support of other nannies. Your nanny does not need to have come from the Special Care Agency. They are happy to introduce any nanny caring for a child needing special care into the group.

Special Care Agency
1st Floor, 45 Pembridge Road, London W11 3HG; 01-221 5894

The Special Care Agency provides help for families with special needs in the form of nannies and mother's helps at all levels of experience to suit the individual family. It also provides help for families who do not have special needs. It offers a personal and thorough service with the added bonus that its staff have a good knowledge of, and many years' experience in, providing the right kind of help for the handicapped.

The Special Care Agency's involvement goes even deeper than supplying the nanny and providing her with a network of like-minded nannies. It organises drinks parties for the nannies, picnics in the summer for nannies and children, and dinners for parents to get them in touch with one another.

The aim is to provide girls who are looking for 'more than just a job'. Its staff are NNEBs; some have more specific qualifications such as physiotherapy or previous employment in special schools. The agency can provide both temporary and permanent staff, those able to take sole charge and those who can take some of the burden off the over-stressed mother. It prides itself on providing a real back-up service to the nannies it places with advice and reassurance about the difficulties of their job and the assurance that being a nanny to a disabled child is a great deal more tiring and demanding, but often in the long run very rewarding.

Specialist minders

Local authorities have their own policies regarding sponsoring children and children with special needs. Haringey in north London offers training for specialist minders, the idea being that specially trained minders will be competent to care for disabled children. Haringey requires preregistration training before they will register a minder as being a specialist minder.

Unfortunately, the difference in remuneration is so far not great enough to be worthwhile, according to the minders I interviewed.

The maximum number of children with special needs a child-minder can care for, including her own, is two. This might be attractive to a minder if her own child is disabled and she can't find anyone to leave him with.

One Haringey minder said she feels the idea is a good one but it must be made financially worthwhile for the minder to take the time to undergo the training and then take on the extra work and responsibility of the care. She feels that, since the minders are no better off financially, there is no incentive for taking on the extra burden. That particular minder likened the situation to taking on sponsored children from the borough Social Services Department who, she said, were always considerably more trouble than other children in her care. She takes in the sponsored children out of the goodness of her heart and is paid less by the borough for working twice as hard.

From the mother of a disabled child's point of view, help must be offered with a view to long-term commitment. The complications of caring for a severely handicapped child, who perhaps can't communicate, has numerous food allergies and serious behaviour problems precludes the use of a carer who comes in once only.

However, the idea is a good one and would be tremendously helpful to parents of children with special needs, even if only for part of the day. Find out if your local authority Social Services Department is planning a similar sort of scheme and with what guidelines.

The London Borough of Brent operates a Share and Care Scheme where, at no cost to the parents, the borough pays another family to provide respite care of a handicapped child.

Societies for disabled children

There are many societies for the disabled giving special help to children. They exist to make the load lighter and the way easier. Do not hesitate to ask for their help.

The Royal Society for Mentally Handicapped Children and Adults (MENCAP)
MENCAP National Centre, 123 Golden Lane, London EC1Y 0RT; 01-253 9433

MENCAP, founded in 1946 as the Association of Parents of Backward Children, has evolved and developed into a society of parents and friends of mentally handicapped people, numbering over 55,000, dedicated to improving the quality of life for the mentally handicapped through public awareness and understanding and providing what is needed.

MENCAP will, on request, send information covering every aspect of managing with a mentally handicapped child. Their fact sheets cover their own activities, holiday services, education and training, insurance and wills and how to ensure that your child will always have care and everything else you have ever wanted to ask. MENCAP itself does not run day-care centres for the young. What it does do is issue a directory called *MENCAP Interlink*. This is aimed at professionals to help them to direct parents of young children with special needs, particularly with learning disabilities, to the support they need. It also gives general information about the provision for children with special needs in London and nationally.

Royal National Institute for the Blind
224 Great Portland Street, London W1N 6AA; 01-388 1266

The RNIB has no policy for or against integration of visually impaired children in normal schools. What is best for the child is the most important concern. Most local education authorities in the UK have specialist services for visually impaired children and increasingly more visually impaired children attend LEA schools close to home. A small team of advisers, all qualified teachers of the blind, work in conjunction with LEA specialist services for the visually impaired. The RNIB acts as back-up for education authorities without their own programmes. Vacation schemes bring together visually impaired children from mainstream schools.

The RNIB runs residential schools for all age groups and academic abilities. Careers and study advisers offer advice and support. There is special provision for multi-handicapped visually impaired children in either one of the schools or in an RNIB school for the multi-handicapped. A range of education courses open to parents to help them to gain a better understanding of their child's problem is also offered.

The RNIB produces some booklets for parents that are essential reading. *Useful Information for Parents of Children with Impaired Vision* advises on who provides help and supplies a glossary of terms that a parent of a child with impaired vision should be familiar with. *Please Help Me* is full of friendly advice on how to make the child's life and understanding of the world about him easier. *One Step at a Time* describes development, helping parents and carers to be prepared and to cope. As well as these booklets, the RNIB supplies information in leaflet form on request.

The Spastics Society
Head Office: 12 Park Crescent, London W1N 4EQ; 01-636 5020

The Spastics Society would give any enquirers the name of their local social worker. The Society has social workers in England and Wales but not in Scotland. For Scotland, apply to:

Scottish Council for Spastics
22 Corstorphine Road, Edinburgh EH12 6HP; 031-337 9876

The Spastics Society publishes a quarterly magazine called *Disability Now* which keeps readers up to date with new legislation and innovations in equipment and management aids for disabled people.

Royal National Institute for the Deaf
105 Gower Street, London WC1E 6AH; 01-387 8033

National Deaf Children's Society
45 Hereford Road, London W2 5AH; 01-229 9272

The National Deaf Children's Society has 130 support groups up and down the country. They find that parents generally come directly to them for advice. The Society puts parents in touch with their local support group and provides advice sheets and booklets on education, health, social services and equipment as well as providing a counselling service.

There is a shortage of social workers specially trained to work with deaf people. As a result many local Social Services Departments don't have a specialised worker in their employ. This situation should improve after 1990 when the Open University will offer a course for qualified social workers who wish to specialise in working with the deaf. The Society stands aside from the policy debate as to which route (signing or lip-reading) is best for deaf children, but rather helps parents to find the right environment and right educational method, letting parents decide which route they want their children to go down.

I have listed the obvious societies and what they offer. There are many others, the names of which are available from the Voluntary Council for Handicapped Children. Below are a few of the societies specifically directed to children's handicaps.

Hyperactive Children's Group
71 Whyke Lane, Chichester, West Sussex PO19 2LD

Founded in 1977 by Sally Bunday, the mother of a hyperactive son, the aim of the Association is to provide information and advice to parents with hyperactive children. It provides a register of parents willing to be put in touch with other parents. Branches exist in various parts of the country and new branches are always being started.

A great deal of their advice is nutritional, based on the work of Ben Feingold in the USA. Dr Feingold recognised that diet could be responsible for some forms of hyperactivity, and his work and research were the inspiration for the founding of the Association.

With membership comes the group's own book, *Hyperactive Children – A Guide to Their Management,* and a journal which comes out three times a year. Membership costs £6.50 for ordinary members (unwaged: £4.50) and £5.50 to professionals who do not want the handbook.

Research is constantly being done on the little understood problem of hyperactivity in children, and children of members of the group often participate in research projects. Behaviour in children has been known to be radically altered by a change in diet, and many children have overcome the worst of their symptoms by their late teens.

National Crossroads
10 Regent's Place, Rugby, Warwickshire CV21 2PN; 0788 73653

The existence of National Crossroads is testimony to the power of the media. The need to care for the individual carers or families of disabled people was portrayed in an incident in the television soap *Crossroads* and resulted in ATV giving £10,000 in 1974 for a pilot project to be set up. Now with funding from the DSS and local health authorities, 143 Crossroads schemes exist nationwide, providing care and relief for the carers. Families can either refer themselves or are referred to Crossroads. Their local scheme assesses the family's needs and works out a package of care. When the carer is feeling at her most tired and vulnerable, a care attendant provides relief, giving the carer a well-earned break. The care attendants are trained professionals, paid by the local scheme, who can do anything the carer can do.

Let's Increase Neuro-Fibromotosis Knowledge (LINK)
1 The Alders, Hanworth, Middlesex TW13 6NV; 01-898 6132

Neuro-fibromotosis is also known as Von Recklinghausen Disease. LINK is a support group for parents.

The National Society for Autistic Children
276 Willesden Lane, London NW2 5RB; 01-451 1114

Association for All Speech Impaired Children (AFASIC)
347 Central Market, Smithfield, London EC1A 9NH; 01-236 3632/ 236 6487

Association for Spina Bifida and Hydrocephalus (ASBAH)
22 Upper Woburn Place, London WC1H 0EP; 01-388 1382

Cystic Fibrosis Research Trust
5 Blyth Road, Bromley, Kent BR1 3RS; 01-464 7211

Chapter 13

Lone Parenting

The single mother's life is the most difficult. Dead tired, all the time, is how single working mothers describe themselves. It isn't just the work and the children; it's the stress of having to make all the decisions alone, worrying about making ends meet, the exhaustion of just coping.

One in three marriages ends in divorce. There are now one million one-parent families in Britain, 81 per cent of which have resulted from death, separation or divorce. Ninety per cent of the lone parents struggling to raise a family on their own are women.

Irretrievable breakdown is the sole cause of divorce in this country. Since 1971, when the law on divorce was changed, there have been no innocent and guilty parties, and no matrimonial offences. Just under 60 per cent of divorcing couples have dependent children. If divorce and marital fertility rates continue at their current level, 20 per cent of all children will experience the divorce of their parents and, subsequently, life with a single, tired, overworked parent struggling to survive. Life is not easy for the single working mother.[1]

Research by the paediatric, social and political science committee at Cambridge University has found that in order to retain a worth-while relationship with an estranged or non-custodial parent, children should spend at least one-quarter of their time with that parent.[2] With only 50 per cent of men keeping contact with their children six months after the divorce, the lone mother has to be both mother and father to her children. Recognising that children with single parents need the input of other adults, single parents are treated favourably as far as places in day nurseries are concerned. There are now so many under-fives with lone parents that it is almost impossible to get other children into a local authority nursery. The places are allocated on the basis of the children's need. Children of lone parents do have a greater need.

1. Statistics from publications of the National Council for One Parent Families.
2. *Children, Separation and Divorce: How Schools can Help*, Rick Rogers, National Council for One Parent Families.

If the children are small and needing full-time care, the lone parent has the choice of paying for alternative care while she works full time, working part time or suffering the consequences of having no personal financial resources. Over 61 per cent of lone mothers are dependent on state benefits to keep their heads above water and only 6 per cent of lone mothers rely on maintenance payments as their only source of family income.

Guides to the benefits the lone parent is entitled to, including Family Credit, One Parent Benefit, the Social Fund and Child Benefit, can be obtained from DSS booklets:

FB8 *Babies and Benefits*
FB27 *Bringing Up Children*
NI 261 *A Guide to Family Credit*

Useful organisations

The single most important back-up the lone parent needs is a supportive circle of friends to provide help. Many lone parents are too proud, embarrassed or even afraid to ask for help.

Tess Fothergill, divorced and left alone in 1970 to bring up two sons, understood that coping with her situation could be made a great deal easier with the support of people in a similar situation. An advert in the newspaper brought in a flood of replies, and Gingerbread, the self-help organisation for lone parents, was born. There are now 300 groups in England and Wales. Gingerbread Scotland is autonomous.

The groups organise activities based on the general aims of:

- providing a regular meeting place for one-parent families;
- providing friendship and companionship;
- giving information and advice as one lone parent to another based on experience, and referring people to professionals if necessary;
- providing moral and emotional support to members;
- providing practical assistance by sharing baby-sitting, taking turns doing the shopping, exchanging labour;
- educating the community about the needs of one-parent families.

Gingerbread groups feel that they are a success if their members can look back on their experience with Gingerbread and say it has made a real difference to their lives. Gingerbread is open to lone parents, both male and female, and to both the custodial and non-custodial parent, although obviously the custodial parent would have the greater need of Gingerbread's activities. The groups are self-supporting and do their best to raise money to support their own activities which are not only confined to the parents' needs. There are lots of children's and teenagers' activities as well.

The national office in London employs an advice worker who is able to give professional advice on social, legal and financial problems including all aspects of housing difficulties and the maze of benefits available to the lone parent. If you phone them they will put you in touch with the group in your area. If you write to them they will send you a list of their helpful publications ranging from Gingerbread's *Social Policy Statement* and *Starting a Creche* to a *Holiday Guide for One Parent Families*.

Gingerbread
National Office, 35 Wellington Street, London WC2E 7BN;
01-240 0953

Gingerbread Scotland
39 Hope Street, Glasgow G2 7DW; 041-248 6840

The National Council for One Parent Families (NCOPF) is a charity and its services are free and confidential. The service includes advice on legal and taxation problems, housing problems, social security and maintenance, and pregnancy counselling. In 1987 they advised over 6000 families, many of whom would have had nowhere else to turn.

Enquiries are dealt with nationally by phone and letter and where appropriate parents are put in touch with local organisations or individuals who can help. One-parent families' advisers also represent lone parents at appeal tribunals. The advice department provides training on legal and welfare rights for one-parent family groups and for professionals on specific issues affecting one-parent families. Their advice service operates from 9.15 am to 5.15 pm on Mondays, Tuesdays, Thursdays and Fridays.

A quarterly newsletter, *One Parent Times*, with news of their campaigns, changes in the law, developments in childcare provision and other useful information, is sent to members.

As a campaigning organisation, NCOPF covers a broad range of issues where the combination of meticulous research and close contact with the experience of one-parent families gets results.

In 1989 NCOPF reports that it is delighted that the government has agreed to pay a £50 childcare allowance to all lone parents taking up a place on a government training scheme.

Constantly seeking new avenues to improve the conditions of the one-parent family, NCOPF has recently instigated a series of training courses in different parts of the country. The purpose of the courses is to help lone parents to develop the personal initiative and resources necessary to deal with the legal and welfare benefit systems and to gain employment.

NCOPF provides a leaflet as a guide to the main benefits for one-parent families. Once you have read through it, the service will advise you on any benefit you think you might be entitled to.

Tax. If you are a lone parent, you claim a single person's allowance and an additional personal allowance. These add up to the same allowance a married man gets.

The tax leaflet, available at your local tax office is IR 29. The tax situation is constantly changing. NCOPF issues leaflets which are updated annually.

NCOPF issues information on tax and legal aid. For £1.40 you can obtain a guide to the legal rights of single mothers encompassing everything from maintenance and inheritance to nationality and custody.

Benefits. NCOPF produces a leaflet which explains *Family Credit*, the weekly cash benefit for parents in low-paid full-time work. The leaflet explains who qualifies to claim, how to claim, gives examples of household budgets and how to work out Family Credit entitlement. It also answers questions regarding other benefits including *Income Support*, which has replaced Supplementary Benefit as the main weekly benefit for day-to-day living expenses for those with little or no income. It is a benefit to help people who do not have enough money to live on.

It provides a leaflet on *Housing Benefit* for council tenants, private tenants or owner-occupiers. It tells you how to work out your Housing Benefit entitlement by explaining all the contributing factors determining whether you qualify and how to get it.

NCOPF is a registered charity dependent on membership fees, donations and legacies. Membership is £2 for lone parents or lone-parent groups, £12 for individuals and £20 for organisations. Membership entitles one to the quarterly newsletter and annual report. Lone parents receive a copy of all their advice publications issued throughout the year.

The National Council for One Parent Families (NCOPF)
255 Kentish Town Road, London NW5 2LX; 01-267 1361

The stress of being a lone parent relates to what is happening at any particular moment. Children are deeply affected by that stress no matter what age. Managing the traumas of adolescence is hard work for the parent on her own. Laying down the law to a teenage son who is a foot taller than you are takes a great deal of patience and skill. All teenagers go through difficult times. It's not easy being a kid and more so in circumstances where your parents are no longer able to live together. Two parents can share the load. One parent has to maintain the energy and resources to deal with every crisis. Two parents can keep tempers below the boiling point. One parent has no one there to arbitrate. Without a catalyst in the household, life for the single parent of teenagers can be emotionally exhausting. The friendships offered by Gingerbread and NCOPF go a long way to help. A problem shared is a problem on its way to being solved.

When a marriage has irretrievably broken down, other agencies are there with advice.

The National Marriage Guidance Council, now called Relate, issues a booklist with a number of small publications on divorce and separation. They also issue a booklet called *Parents are Forever* which offers brief guidelines of behaviour for parents in regard to their children and their relationship with them after divorce.

Look in the telephone directory for the National Marriage Guidance office in your area or phone the main headquarters nearest you.

Relate (England)
Herbert Gray College, Little Church Street, Rugby CV21 3AP; 0788 73241

Relate (Northern Ireland)
76 Dublin Road, Belfast ET2 7HP; 0232 323454

The Scottish Marriage Guidance Council
26 Frederick Street, Edinburgh EH2 2JR; 031-225 5006

Another organisation in Scotland is Parents Forever Scotland. It is a registered charity and a self-help organisation for fathers and mothers who no longer live with their children. Its aims include: 'to help parents maintain contact by providing support and counselling for non-custodial parents; to encourage all efforts at conciliation in the interest of the family.'

Parents Forever Scotland
Community House, 47–48 Greenlaw Crescent, Glenrothes, Fife KY6 1JQ; 0592 755458

Parents Forever Scotland issues five leaflets giving advice in various areas of difficulty at the time of divorce. The leaflets address the problems of *Access for the Non-custodial Parent, Custody, Mediation: Using the Conciliation Service, Selecting a Solicitor and Legal Aid* and *Maintaining your Child.* If you send an A4-size stamped self-addressed envelope and a small donation in postage stamps to help with production costs, PFS will gladly forward the five leaflets to you.
    Here are some other useful addresses:

Divorce, Conciliation and Advisory Service
Office 2, 38 Ebury Street, London SW1 0LU; 01-730 2422

Scottish Association Family Conciliation Service
40 Shandwick Place, Edinburgh EH2 4RT; 031-220 1610

National Family Conciliation Council
34 Milton Road, Swindon, Wiltshire SN1 5JA; 0793 618486

Jewish Marriage Guidance Council
23 Ravenshurst Avenue, London NW4 4EL; 01-203 6311

Jewish Marriage Guidance Council
Levi House, Bury Old Road, Manchester M8 6FX; 061-740 5764

Catholic Marriage Advisory Council (CMAC)
23 Kensington Square, London W8 5HN; 01-937 3781

Scotland: Scottish CMAC
194 Clyde Street, Glasgow G1 4JY; 041-204 1239

Ireland: Irish CMAC
All Hallows College, Drumcondra, Dublin 9, Republic of Ireland; 0001 375649

National Stepfamily Association
162 Tenison Road, Cambridge CB1 2DP; 0223 460312
For counselling service ring: 0223 460313

National Stepfamily Association (Scotland)
10 Abbotsford Crescent, Edinburgh EH10 5DY; 031-447 4131

Bibliography

Julia Brannen and Peter Moss *New Mothers at Work – Employment and Childcare* (Unwin Paperbacks)

Bronwen Cohen *Caring for Children. Services and Policies for Childcare and Equal Opportunities in the United Kingdom.* Report for the European Commission's Childcare Network. (The Commission of the European Communities)

Irene Fox *Private Schools and Public Issues – The Parent's View* (Macmillan, 1985)

Robert Goffee and Richard Scase *Women in Charge: The Experience of Female Entrepreneurs* (George Allen & Unwin, 1985)

Frances O'Grady and Heather Wakefield *Women, Work and Maternity – The Inside Story* (Maternity Alliance)

Michael Rutter *Maternal Deprivation – Reassessed* (Penguin)

Sirgay Sanger and John Kelly *The Woman Who Works, The Parent Who Cares:* Making Work a Positive Force in the Life of Your Child (Transworld)

Sue Sharpe *Double Identity: Lives of Working Mothers* (Penguin, 1984)

The Employer's Guide to Childcare (Working Mothers Association)

The Working Mothers Handbook (Working Mothers Association)

Further reading from Kogan Page

Changing Your Job After 35: The Daily Telegraph Guide, 6th edition, Godfrey Golzen and Philip Plumbley, 1988

Getting There: Jobhunting for Women, Margaret Wallis, 1987

Great Answers to Tough Interview Questions, 2nd edition, Martin John Yate, 1988

Leadership Skills for Women, Marilyn Manning and Patricia Haddock, 1989

Moving On from Teaching, Caroline Elton, 1987

Moving to the Country, David Green, 1990

Part-Time Work, 2nd edition, Judith Humphries, 1986

Returning to Work: A Practical Guide for Women, Alec Reed, 1989

Splitting Up: A Legal and Financial Guide to Separation and Divorce, David Green, 1989

Starting to Teach: Surviving and Succeeding in the Classroom, Anthony D Smith, 1988

Index